Performance Skiing

Performance Skiing

Training and Techniques to Make You a Better Alpine Skier

George Thomas

Stackpole Books

Copyright © 1992 by Stackpole Books

Published by
STACKPOLE BOOKS
Cameron and Kelker Streets
P.O. Box 1831
Harrisburg, PA 17105

Printed in the United States of America

First Edition

10 9 8 7 6 5 4 3 2

Cover design by Caroline Miller
Cover photo by Roger Barnett

Library of Congress Cataloging-in-Publication Data

Thomas, George, 1949–
    Performance skiing : training and techniques to make you a better
alpine skier / George Thomas. — 1st ed.
        p.   cm.
    Includes bibliographical references (p.   ) and index.
    ISBN 0-8117-3026-3 : $15.95
    1. Downhill skiing—Training. 2. Physical fitness. 3. Exercise.
I. Title.
GV854.85.T48   1992   92-3586
796.93′5—dc20   CIP

The will to win is nothing without the will to prepare.

——Juma Ikanga
New York Marathon winner

Contents

Acknowledgments

The nice thing about skiing is that no matter how good you think you are, someone can always show you something new. I would particularly like to thank Rick Reid, coach of the Crystal Mountain Alpine Club, and his assistants, Alan Lauba, Lloyd Scroggins, and Dave Mahalko. Chris Thompson, coach of the Pacific Northwest PSIA Demo Team, and Demo Team member Kelley Yackley, also provided much technical information. Thanks also to Tim Ross, director of the U.S. Ski Coaches Association, for the excellent symposium. Roy Stevenson, M.S.P.E., helped clarify various concepts related to physical fitness.

For help with the chapter on equipment, I would like to thank Jim Deines of Precision Ski, Blake Lewis of the K2 Ski Corporation, Jay Larsen of Montana Sports, Brent Amsbury of World Cup Ski Tuning, Dave Longmuir of Swix, Kelly Timmons of Flamingo Sports, and Steve Forsythe of Sturtevant's Sports.

Additionally, John Erben, editor of *Sports Northwest* magazine, and Roger Barnett helped with photography. I thank Mark Salverda for his illustrations.

Special thanks to Timberline Lodge, with the best summer race training and skiing in North America, for its hospitality.

ONE

The Challenge of Skiing Today

PERFORMANCE, used as an adjective for skiing, like *cutting edge* or *state of the art*, is grossly overworked by modern advertising. Unfortunately, there are few other terms to properly convey that to which so many skiers aspire.

Throughout this book, you'll encounter the terms *performance skiing* and *performance skier*. What is this and who is doing it?

There are lots of good skiers, but to the performance skier, the sport is more than just recreation. It is a lifestyle and personal expression. Such a skier is always looking for another insight into the art. On the hill, he is constantly challenged by terrain and conditions. When others are scampering out of the fog, rain, or blizzard, he is out there putting himself to the test. Anything outside of earning a living that requires a day or two away from the sport is deferred until spring.

Skiing has matured dramatically in the past two decades. Some regret a certain loss of the rugged backwoods ethic, but despite the neon glitz of skiing today, the limits of performance have never been higher and the challenge has never been greater.

Technique

Twenty years ago, the ski schools of different nations took different approaches. The merits of French technique over Austrian, and vice versa, were debated, though in retrospect the differences were not all that great. Today, there is no difference in the way the best skiers from Sweden or Italy ski compared with the Japanese, Yugoslavs, or anyone else.

The homogenizing of technique throughout the world is primarily due to physical constraints. The ski operates most efficiently by applying force in specific ways. The physical principles are much better understood today. In the United States, ski instructors are organized through the Professional Ski Instructors of America, which has developed rigorous technical standards for certification. PSIA contributes to the evolution of technique and methodology by participating in Interski, a quadrennial international gathering of the best instructors from every alpine country.

Coaches training tomorrow's Olympians further develop their skills through continuing education provided by the U.S. Ski Coaches Association, which has its own standards for certification. As the USSCA is an adjunct to the U.S. Ski Team, its program is derived directly from the methods and techniques used by skiers on the World Cup tour.

Technology

Another major factor in skiing today is the tremendous potential created by technology. Many common materials such as Kevlar and ceramic fibers did not exist a few years ago, and are used to reinforce, lighten, and enhance properties of skis. Twenty years ago, I visited the Dynamic ski factory in France. The ramshackle building was staffed by great old guys with rough hands, wearing berets and smoking hand-rolled cigarettes. The pride they had in their skis was apparent with autographed pictures of Jean-Claude Killy and other French greats hanging on the wall. Today, the pride is still there, but the plant is modern and controlled by computer.

Modern ski design employs sophisticated technology and sensitive laboratory testing. Internal and external dampers are tuned to allow performance-enhancing vibrations but inhibit others. Sintered bases and stone grinding give skis a gliding surface unattainable a few years back. At the K2 company's plant on Vashon Island, Washington, a giant braider weaves a fiberglass "sock" around laminated cores. Depending on the characteristics desired, the braid can be changed and fabrics can be added. Skis are more stable than ever before, yet they are also more nimble. They can glide at far higher speeds, but turn on a dime.

Current boots transmit forces much better than ones a few years old, but at the same time fewer skiers are afflicted with the bone spurs that used to be common. Boot heaters provide comfort, and bindings, previously only for safety, are now designed to contribute to performance by working in sync with the ski.

Clothing has made a quantum jump as well. Fabrics are not only waterproof and breathable, but some now actually generate heat from sunlight.

Ski Areas

Ski areas contour hills in the summer and employ fleets of grooming vehicles and snow-making equipment to turn many a down-home run into a snow autobahn in the winter. The high-speed detachable quad lift has created a skier who only grudgingly rides a conventional double, whereas five years ago, he was happy if the line didn't exceed forty-five minutes. A few years ago, twenty runs in a day was pressing it; today, you can get in thirty runs before closing time.

At the 1989 FIS World Championships in Vail and Beaver Creek, Colorado, part of the downhill was sculpted into a kind of luge run. For the 1992 Winter Olympics in France, about $9.2 million was spent on a slalom stadium, complete with underground TV wiring and pipes for snow-making machines.

The Skier Revisited

With all these developments in the last few years, technology has brought skiing full circle—the individual is back in the spotlight. It's as if the skier of the 1990s has been given the keys to the Starship Enterprise. Can he handle it?

Most skiers are happy to slide around the mountain a couple of times a year. They're important because they provide the capital and demand for the skiing industry. But those who really want to take advantage of what's available need to ask, Am I strong enough to move up the performance ladder? Do I know how to get the most out of my equipment?

Snow Country magazine reported, "Pivot skidders outnumber all other skiers today. They can be seen on any hill, any day of the season, throwing their skis to one side and then to the other as they skid down the mountainside, often just at (or over) the hairy edge of control." To take full control of the technology advantages available to him, this skier must reassess his physical and technical abilities.

This book is not for the beginner. One of the most important ways to improve your skiing is by getting in better physical condition, so most of it is devoted to that. Physical training is no longer separate from skiing. Just as buying a lift ticket and waxing your skis are essential, conditioning is necessary for the serious skier.

What the Indianapolis 500 is to General Motors for its research and development, World Cup racing is to recreational skiing worldwide. Technique, equipment, and fashion are all put to the test, so what racers do and the average weekend warrior does differ only in degree. And while everyone can benefit from developing better technique, at all levels of skiing (particularly the upper end) the rule is that better skiing comes from better conditioning.

All national ski teams now have rigorous physical fitness programs; the U.S. team has several year-round conditioning coaches. Because all the World Cup athletes are in such excellent shape, it's difficult to make a difference by working out harder. This wasn't always the case; Bob Beattie's 1964 Olympic team, which won four medals, went through conditioning programs that were unknown elsewhere. The French team of the late 1960s dominated racing, largely because of tough physical training. The "Crazy Canucks" of the late '70s and early '80s ruled the downhill because of their awesome physical shape.

You may never have the slightest desire to chase a gate, but performance skiing is never something that's handed to you just because you wear a spiffy powder suit. Much comes from the condition of the motor under all the stretch neon and Gore-Tex.

The other part of the performance equation is technique. Instructing on the hill is challenging; somehow the teacher must press the right buttons in the learner. More daunting is to try to impart skiing knowledge from a page. There is no feedback, and because skiing is a flowing, sensual activity, the unrelenting question becomes how to best isolate the little nuances and dynamics and try to blend them into a seamless whole.

A lot of people hate to read instruction manuals, so how could this knowledge be presented to appeal to impulsive skiers? Rather than present the standard wedge-to-parallel sequence, this book suggests different exercises you can try, on easy and difficult terrain. They are designed to improve balance, timing, and coordination that you can integrate into your skiing. The chapter on technique should give you a good intellectual framework, and the drills that follow will help enhance the skills.

To some, this book may appear to encourage fast and reckless skiing. Fast, yes; reckless, no. To ski really fast requires great control. Risk is inherent in skiing, and those unwilling to assume responsibility for their actions don't belong in the mountains. North American skiing areas, in an attempt to limit their legal liability, have greatly restricted where skiers can go and what they can do. For most people, that's probably a good idea. But if you want to develop a special skill and the responsibility that goes with it, this book's for you.

TWO

Physical Fitness for Skiers

EVERY FALL, the skiing magazines publish articles on fitness, and most of the advice is good. Because of their scope, periodicals tend to suggest specific exercises but don't say how or why they apply to skiing. Here is a brief look at the principles of fitness and conditioning and how they relate to the sport. With some understanding of how your body responds to exercise, you can better evaluate your routines and improve your fitness for skiing.

Components of Physical Fitness

When we watch sports stars in action, we envy their athleticism and admire their fitness. Their chosen sport has its own demands, and each athlete is superbly adapted to them. All athletes have some common attributes, yet they all differ. What has taken them to the summits of their sports, and what is important to skiers?

Elmar Kornexl, a professor at the University of Innsbruck, Austria, conducted a study in the late 1970s and found a number of traits important for alpine skiing; jumping dexterity, explosive leg strength, strength and leg muscle endurance, static strength of the knee and hip muscles, dynamic strength of the hip flexors, local dynamic endurance of the hip and abdominal muscles, elasticity in lateral foot-to-foot hopping, and reaction speed. These are good to keep in mind, but we can examine more general components of fitness that are crucial to top skiers.

Performance skiing puts a premium on every constituent of physical fitness. No single exercise will be complete preparation for skiing. Quite simply, at the upper levels, you must be in better overall shape in order to ski better. Here are nine topics related to your physical ability.

AGE. Past the age of twenty-six or so, optimum athletic performance declines. Nevertheless, precluding any joint or conditioning problems, a skillful skier should be able to keep up with the strongest youngsters well into his forties.

In his last year of racing, Karl Schranz won three tough World Cup downhills at age thirty-three. Ingemar Stenmark also won his last World Cup race at thirty-three. It's as much an attitude as a physical state. When asked how it felt to be the oldest downhiller on the World Cup tour at the 1989 FIS World Championships, Peter Mueller of Switzerland replied, "I'd rather be old and fast than young and slow."

The heart's pumping ability declines about 8% per year after the twenties, and muscles lose 3% to 5% of their strength each decade. By age seventy-five, you have about half the physical capacity you had at twenty. Regular lifetime exercise has been shown to slow the decline in athletic performance by about half. Particularly important for skiers, exercise can halt or slow joint deterioration that often accompanies aging.

An important gauge of fitness is heart rate, of which more will be said later. The rule of thumb is that your maximum rate is 220 minus your age. For anyone over fifty, a physician should conduct a treadmill test to determine maximum heart rate and any cardiac problems.

AEROBIC-ANAEROBIC CAPACITY. Aerobic condition usually refers to athletic performance in low-intensity, extended activity and anaerobic to a high-intensity, brief effort. In a more specific sense, aerobic (with oxygen) and anaerobic (without oxygen) refer to the body's two means of converting food to energy and its application.

Regular exercise can signifi-
cantly slow the steady
decline of physical capacity
that starts at age twenty for
the average person.

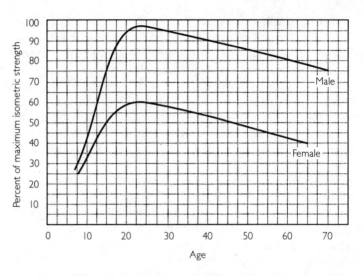

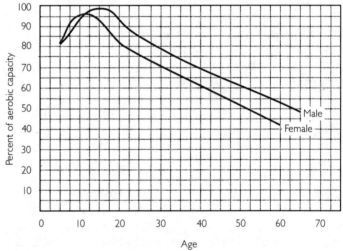

When discussing a body's aerobic fitness, we actually refer to the efficiency of the entire cardiopulmonary system and the ability of the muscles to utilize oxygen. Improvement of aerobic capacity means enhancing cellular biochemistry, lung capacity, and heart stroke volume; lowering the resting pulse rate and cholesterol level; and developing more capillary permeation. A guideline for aerobic fitness training would be to gradually work toward sixty minutes of exercise during which your pulse was elevated to 60%

to 90% of your maximum heart rate, three to five days per week. There will be more on heart rates in the next chapter.

The anaerobic system refers to how well you convert fuel to muscle energy in the absence of sufficient oxygen for aerobic metabolism. An anaerobically fit athlete can tolerate high levels of lactic acid (the by-product of anaerobic metabolism) in his muscles while continuing to perform. Anaerobic training improves short-term endurance and the output of skeletal muscles.

Though data are limited, there is evidence that heavy aerobic training can reduce your maximum strength potential if you are training for both endurance and strength. However, strength training has not been shown to inhibit aerobic endurance.

Performance skiers should pay attention to these energy pathways. The physical demands of performance skiing require great anaerobic fitness. Dr. George Twardokens, professor of kinesiology at the University of Nevada, suggests at least 20% of alpine skiing is anaerobic. Typical heart rates range from 160 to 200 in racers and 130 to 170 in recreational skiers.

In the last two years, members of the U.S. Ski Team have reduced the time devoted to aerobic exercise and spent more on high-intensity, short-duration anaerobic work.

Before you bag the jogging and start doing intervals, remember that elite skiers score much higher aerobically than even most serious recreational runners. Also, remember that good aerobic exercise helps your body tolerate the physical stress of anaerobic work, such as sprinting 440s.

Performance skiing does have important aerobic requirements, and all skiers need better-than-average endurance. Since it's a high-altitude sport, smokers and those with poor aerobic capacity are seriously disadvantaged. Aerobic fitness also helps rapid recovery from oxygen debt.

FLEXIBILITY. This is easily the most neglected component of performance skiing. Interestingly, while hard skiing can enhance fitness (such as leg strength), flexibility is the only component that will diminish if not worked on specifically. As the season goes on, many skiers feel stuck on a performance plateau. Frequently, this is because of a reduction in flexibility; all the muscles that run down the back, the back of the legs, and the calves become short and tight throughout a season. Lack of flexibility also increases the possibility of injury.

Flexibility is simply a joint's range of motion. It is determined by how much your muscles can stretch beyond their normal resting length and return (elasticity); the maximum length of a muscle, which is about 60% beyond its resting length (extensibility); the health of the connective tissue surrounding a joint; and the body's protective stretch (myotatic) reflex. This last, the reflexive contraction a muscle makes when it is stretched, protects the muscle from unexpected strains. Jerky bouncing movement (ballistic stretching) expands and contracts the muscle quickly, risking tears in the muscle tissue. Slow, steady stretching, on the other hand, allows the muscle to extend fully and more safely.

Some skiers have maintained that weight training reduces flexibility. They sacrifice strength to gain flexibility. The opposite is actually the case. By stretching and using resistance through a complete range of motion, flexibility will increase along with strength. Look at gymnasts to see how strength and flexibility work together.

COORDINATION. Pat your head and rub your stomach at the same time for about ten seconds. Simple, right? Now, do it again, then quickly switch hands. Not so easy. How long does it take to figure this one out?

The ability to learn a skilled movement is a measure of coordination. Coordination is difficult to quantify because it is so skill-specific. You may be an awesome skier, but that does not make you a good platform diver.

As the word implies, coordination integrates action and sensory awareness and is developed primarily between the ages of six and fifteen. Adults who were not exposed to motor skill challenges in their youth have particular difficulty learning new movement patterns.

Werner Margreiter, a former Austrian team racer

and Austrian women's team coach, said, "The structure of motor skills consists of five areas: balance [as the central factor], responsiveness, sense of direction, ability to differentiate, and rhythm." The U.S. Ski Team Training Manual states that coordination "is related to the individual's insight into the nature of a skill, general kinesthetic sensibility and control, the ability to visualize spatial relationships [depth perception], and judgment concerning time, height, distance, and direction." Agility also figures in.

Everyone has motor skills; they are needed to walk across a room. Coordination is highly refined in athletes so they can master complex movements quickly and easily. The technical aspects of skiing highly depend on motor skills—balancing on one foot or the other, twisting, and moving up and down at high speed. Any skill is learned by breaking movement down into subroutines, then combining these practiced elements into continuous movement.

Even if you were a basket case until late in life does not mean you are a terminal klutz. You will enhance your skiing by challenging yourself with other skill movements. A number of these exercises are offered later.

BALANCE. This is your ability to maintain an equilibrium. In skiing, this is done on a moving base. Skiers don't balance on the ski as much as against it as it moves through a turn. Beginning skiers must find a neutral balanced body position that is not perpendicular to a flat surface but perpendicular to the slope. It becomes more difficult the steeper the hill becomes. At every waking moment, muscles, senses, and nervous system are keeping our bodies in balance. Even sitting in a chair, a part of your brain and the muscles in your neck and shoulders are keeping your head balanced over your torso.

Balance is specific to what you are doing, whether it's tightrope walking, rock climbing, skateboarding, or balance-beam tumbling. In skiing, it has to do with how far you move out of a stable equilibrium before your brain informs the muscles and then the speed with which you respond.

Balance is related to agility in that quicker countering moves are needed when your base of support is small. Think of your body as a stack of boxes. Arrange each so that the line of gravity passes through the center of each box. Keep your weight over your base of support. Keep your base wide in the direction of travel or the direction from which you will encounter a force, but do not overextend. Keep your center of gravity close to your base by keeping your hips low. Balance with your arms up and out to the side. Keep your eyes focused on one spot and your head and shoulders level.

If you do all of this and are short and stocky to begin with, you can't fall over. Balance-enhancing exercises will be discussed later.

AGILITY. This concerns how fast you can change direction of movement. How quickly your muscles can contract—your reaction time—depends a lot on whether you inherited fast- or slow-twitch muscle fibers. But agility can also be improved with training. Agile athletes also tend to be flexible and have a high strength-to-weight ratio.

STRENGTH. Strength is your ability to exert force against resistance, and is usually measured through one normal movement. Any physical action requires some strength, but in skiing, a lot of force is applied against a lot of resistance. It has been estimated that elite skiers momentarily support as much as 500 pounds on one leg in some turns.

Strength is increased by overloading muscles with progressively greater resistance. This resistance can be applied isometrically, isotonically, or isokinetically. Isometric resistance involves the muscle tensing against an immovable object, such as when you sit against a wall without a chair. Isotonic resistance entails forced movement of the body part, such as when you use weights or exercise machines. This kind of resistance actually involves two muscular contractions—concentric, in which the muscle shortens, and eccentric, or negative, in which the muscle lengthens while effort is made to resist the movement. In a dumbbell curl, muscles contract concentrically as you raise the weight to your chest, and eccentrically as you slowly lower the weight. Isokinetic resistance is found primarily on specialized equipment like a Cybex machine, which has variable resistance and a governor that allows movement at only a selected speed. Depending on the preset speed, this type of machine can train either fast-twitch or slow-twitch fibers.

Though there are moments of isometric resistance in skiing, isometric exercise does not increase strength much at angles of force different from those used in the exercise. It also increases the load on the cardiovascular system and raises blood pressure by occluding blood vessels when the muscle is contracted. Isotonic training through a full range of motion is more effective in developing the strength and flexibility needed for performance skiing. Occasional negative (eccentric) training provides maximal resistance and overload. For instance, have a spotter help raise more weight than you can bench press unaided. From the top of the lift, resist as much as possible while the bar settles down to your chest.

According to Tim LaVallee, former director of the U.S. Ski Coaches Association, exercise load should be about 85% of your one-repetition maximum weight (1RM), the most weight you can lift once. By doing five or six reps for three to five sets, you can achieve optimum strength gains. Be sure to have someone spot if you decide to determine your RM.

Contrary to what some believe, strength training through a full range of motion, plus stretching, in-

For overall balanced fitness, skiers should develop their upper-body strength as well as leg strength. Karen Kendall of the U.S. Ski Team spots teammate Stephanie Palmer on a set of incline presses.

creases flexibility. Increased strength also increases speed.

Women have often avoided weight training for fear of developing bulging muscles. This is changing because of new definitions of beauty—just look at Cory Everson, former Miss Olympia—but more so because of the understanding that, even with regular weight training, most women will not develop huge muscles.

POWER. *Power* and *strength* are often used interchangeably in skiing, but there is a difference, especially for performance skiers. To be powerful, you must be strong, but power involves time—how much force you can exert in a given period. Obviously, there's an element of power no matter how slowly you exert force, but in skiing, we're concerned with quickness and speed. In power training, you also train your central nervous system.

Like gymnastics or judo, performance skiing is a power sport. We all enjoy lazy trips down ballroom-groomed runs from time to time, but when you're cooking, you want strong legs working fast. James Fixx, in his book *Maximum Sports Performance*, described tests performed in 1970 on subjects who exercised at slow speeds. Though they showed strength gains against resistance at slow speeds, negligible gains were seen during higher-speed exercises. This means skiers should devote strength training to dynamic lifting. LaVallee recommends power training between 50% and 70% of your RM, which allows ten to fifteen reps in three to five sets.

MUSCLE ENDURANCE. This is your ability to perform muscular work at high levels over prolonged periods. Traditionally, athletes have conditioned by building a good aerobic base, then incorporating strength training and finally working on power. Recently, athletes in many sports, including skiing, have turned this concept around by first developing strength, then power and endurance. As Dr. Stephen Johnson said in an article in *Winning* magazine, "Look at it this way: Endurance is merely the ability to be strong and powerful for an extended period of time. You cannot expect to be strong and powerful for minutes or hours if you aren't strong and powerful to start. Any program which emphasizes endurance without addressing your need for strength and power is doomed to failure with respect to taking you to the top of the performance pyramid."

If you ski at an area with a high-speed quad lift, you might get twenty or more long runs in a day, which should leave you dragging. Performance skiers will expend energy similar to an equivalent number of 440s, 880s, or 1,500-meter runs. The point is that it's not just a matter of developing strength and power, but being able to apply this power many times throughout the day. Because exercise is also specific to duration, as your workouts progress, you'll want to increase the number of repetitions and intervals to build endurance.

Principles of Training

OVERLOAD. If you progressively increase the physical demands made on your body, it will become stronger and more efficient, up to your age and genetic limits. You can induce this training effect by an increase in intensity, duration, or frequency. You increase the intensity of a workout by reducing the time allotted for a given amount of work, which improves strength and power. If you increase the duration of work, you enhance endurance, but the load will need to be reduced accordingly. Increased exercise frequency reduces the amount of time for recovery between workouts.

As you become better conditioned, the amount of work you need for incremental strength or endurance gains increases. Too much intensity, duration, and especially frequency without adequate recovery time will cause injuries or overtraining syndrome. Not all parts of your body adapt to increased stress at the same rate. After starting a new conditioning program, your muscles become stronger and can exert more force, bones become denser, and ligaments and tendons become thicker and more elastic. Connective tissue does not respond as quickly as muscle, however. Without allowing tendons and ligaments time to catch up with the muscles, continued exertion can cause joint and tendon injury.

SPECIFICITY. Specificity simply means that the results of any exercise program are specific to it; you get what you train for. Conditioning is specific to muscle groups, range of motion, speed of movements, duration, and energy output. Lots of bench presses, squats, and curls will have little influence on endurance for long-distance running or cycling. Conversely, the hour runs or five-hour bike rides do nothing to increase the number of plates you can put on the bar at the gym.

What complicates preseason conditioning is that there are no single or few exercises that duplicate all the demands of skiing. Consequently, you often hear, "The only way to get in shape for skiing is to ski." This notion makes me cringe. If all you did was ski, before long, muscle imbalances would reduce flexibility and lead to injury. Since you would soon adapt to the normal stresses of skiing, your performance would level off because at some point you no longer overload your system. You can improve your preseason with several activities, each emphasizing one or more skiing requirements. Participate in sports that require short bursts of exertion, balance, agility, and new motor skills.

My understanding of specificity became painfully clear several years ago. I had devoted all of my fall exercise time to preparing for a marathon, which I ran in 3:20, soon followed by a thirty-eight-minute 10K. I felt "fit," but after three days of hard season-opening skiing, I was so stiff and sore that I hobbled around for several days, sustained by ice and aspirin.

VARIETY. One of the biggest problems with conditioning programs is monotony. Most athletes like to work out, and hard. But few can tolerate weeks or months of the same routines. It's boring and can overemphasize some muscles and movements.

Through general conditioning, sports participation, and learning new skills, you develop a broad athletic base. This is important for skiers because they learn adaptability. You'll get more out of your skiing because you have a richer spectrum of talents from which to draw.

Some say you have to give up other sports to excel at one. This may apply at the highest level of a sport, but skiers are notorious overachievers. Steve Hegg was a national downhill champion in 1982 and won an Olympic gold medal in cycling in 1984. John Atkins, former U.S. Ski Team conditioning coach, said that Marc Girardelli, one of the half-dozen fastest 440 sprinters in Austria, spends much of his summers at track meets. Canadian downhiller Rob Boyd joins other skiing luminaries such as Eva Twardokens, Beth Madsen, Monique Pelletier, and Alan Lauba at the Columbia River Gorge for some serious board sailing in the summer. Phil Mahre never felt that he was the strongest athlete on the World Cup circuit, but credited the variety of sports that he and his brother, Steve, pursued for their athletic excellence.

Skill and strength sports reinforce skiing skills. For the serious skier, they also reinforce athletic attitude and self-confidence.

RECOVERY. Conditioning is based on overload, which involves breaking down your system (the catabolic cycle) and then rebuilding it in a stronger state (the anabolic cycle). Strength and power training severely stress your body in a short period, so allow sufficient rest between workouts for your body to rebuild. Regular workouts should include training days with reduced loads to offset hard days.

For most hard exercise sessions involving anaerobic or strength training, forty-eight to seventy-two hours are needed. With a good training program, you will see rapid strength gains in as little as eight weeks by working out no more than three or four times per week. For those who want to do more work and who spend more time in the gym, split your routines so that you work your upper body one day and lower the next.

Over time, overloading without adequate recovery will cause "overtraining," or a decline in athletic performance. Dan Graetzer of the University of Utah's Peak Academy said that it was estimated that 65% of all elite athletes overtrain at some point. The overtrained athlete's standards drop; he feels tired and sore, and needs more recovery time. Chronic overtraining can cause weight loss, increase susceptibility to disease, disturb sleep, and spur emotional problems. One to two weeks of rest can cure short-term overtraining, but severe cases may require a rest of up to six months.

Overtraining is most noticeably indicated by an elevated resting heart rate taken upon waking in the morning. A blood chemistry analysis can verify this.

Conditioned, rested athletes experience less depression, anger, and confusion and are more vigorous than the general population. Overtrained athletes feel energy levels lower than the general population and experience more tension, irritability, depression, and fatigue.

MOTIVATION. This springs from many sources, especially creation of goals. The more clearly you can define your goals, the easier it is to apply yourself. For ski racers, goal setting can be easy, with timed runs, race results, and seeding lists as feedback. Debbie Armstrong, who won an Olympic gold medal in 1984 in giant slalom, credits much of her success to setting attainable goals, immediate and long-term, over a number of years.

For recreational skiers, goal setting is somewhat more difficult and may be irrelevant. After all, you don't dance just to see who can get to the other side of the floor the fastest. By setting goals to improve overall fitness, however, you can also quickly improve your skiing skills. As the ad says, "Just do it."

THE PATHWAYS OF POWER. When you understand why you are doing something, the how becomes a little easier. Let's look at how your body creates energy. Just as certain exercises work on specific muscles, certain activities develop specific energy production systems in your body.

Metabolism, the conversion of food to energy, permits life: cells grow and divide, glands secrete, nerves conduct, and muscles contract. Here we are concerned with the action of muscle cells.

Food is not converted directly into energy; rather, it is used to create a complex chemical compound called adenosine triphosphate (ATP). Muscles work by breaking ATP down into smaller compounds. Breaking of the molecular bond releases a tiny spark of energy that the cell needs to perform its work. The amount of ATP required by a person in twenty-four hours can equal half to all of his body mass. Consequently, ATP is not stored, but is produced as needed. Almost as fast as it breaks down, ATP regenerates, and its reconstruction requires energy.

ATP can be re-created in three ways, depending

upon the demands being placed on the muscles. These energy pathways are known as the ATP-PC system, the lactic acid system, and the oxygen or aerobic system. The first two are anaerobic.

ATP-PC system. This is the fastest method of energy production. In a flurry of intense activity, muscles break down the tiny amount of ATP present in their fibers. Also present in the cell is phosphocreatine (PC), which breaks down, too. The energy released from the PC bond allows ATP to re-form for another cycle of muscular contraction. Because the ATP-PC system is so fast, it provides sudden energy, such as that needed for a short sprint. Because muscles can store only a small amount of PC, the supply is exhausted within five to eight seconds. PC is regenerated after about one minute of rest. When you run a forty-yard dash or throw a shot put, you rely on the ATP-PC system. If you continue to exercise, the ATP-LA system begins its work.

Lactic acid system. Lactic acid (LA) is a by-product of the breakdown of carbohydrates (variously called sugar, glucose, and starch) stored as glycogen in muscle tissue and the liver. As muscles rapidly run out of PC, they turn to glucose stored in the bloodstream and glycogen in the liver. This system also works very quickly. It is inefficient, however, in that it only returns 6% of the available energy from carbohydrates. In a complex process, enzymes transform glycogen into pyruvic acid, hydrogen, and ATP.

When prolonged activity exceeds the rate at which oxygen can cleanse the system of lactic acid, pyruvic acid joins with hydrogen and forms lactic acid. The rapid buildup raises the acidity of the cell environment, inhibiting enzymes that break down glycogen. Muscular contraction grinds to a halt within two and a half to three minutes. As aerobic activity takes over, built-up lactic acid is oxidized as fuel in the muscle or, during rest, is reconverted into glycogen in the liver.

One generally accepted theory is that lactic acid interacts with the buffering systems in the blood, increasing the production of carbon dioxide, which in turn stimulates faster breathing. If you are breathing normally and take off skiing from a dead stop, the anaerobic ATP-PC and ATP-LA systems act like a kick

Your body produces energy by forming and breaking down ATP during the metabolic process. Note that oxygen enters this process only during its final stages.

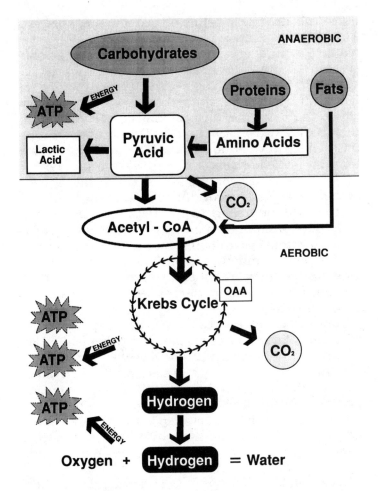

starter, allowing the body to perform at high levels until faster respiration allows the aerobic system to catch up.

Aerobic system. This system is used the most. During normal activity, demands aren't great enough to fully activate the anaerobic systems. The trade-off is that the aerobic system releases a much larger portion of energy available from food; it is about thirteen times more efficient than anaerobic metabolism. It also is long-lasting.

As in the ATP-LA system, glycogen is broken down, but here oxygen cleanses the system. Pyruvic acid is converted into an intermediate compound that produces more ATP. Water and carbon dioxide also are formed and are expelled through the lungs. At this stage, even more energy is released for ATP reconstruction.

The aerobic system is so efficient because it is cyclical. An end product (oxaloacetic acid) necessary to re-start the cycle is produced.

A very precise test of aerobic capacity is performed using a motorized treadmill or bicycle ergometer with the athlete breathing through a face mask for gas analysis. Though elite skiers are tested every year, for most people, this procedure is expensive, uncomfortable, and unnecessary.

The energy spectrum. During any activity, all three systems described above provide some energy. The intensity and duration of activity, however, define which system provides the most energy. Astrand and Rodahl show how, in a sixty-minute maximal work test, at the ten-second mark, 85% of the energy yield was anaerobic; at the two-minute mark, both systems were equal; and at the sixty-minute mark, 2% was anaerobic and 98% was aerobic.

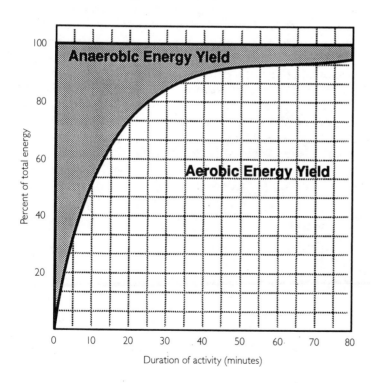

All athletes draw energy from both pathways, but alpine skiers, with their short bursts of intense effort, make greater demands upon their anaerobic systems than their aerobic.

In the chair lift, the aerobic system maintains life functions. As you push off the chair and start down the hill, the ATP-PC system gives a little boost. Bouncing down the first steep pitch through the moguls, you'll rapidly activate the ATP-LA system. If you stop, you will be breathing hard to repay the oxygen debt to your system. As you ski easily over the groomed slopes heading toward the lodge, you are breathing deeply but oxygen consumption is in step with aerobic metabolism.

The harder you can exercise without relying on the ATP-LA system and experiencing the withering effects of lactic acid buildup, the better. This is important for performance skiers, as runs typically are surges of short, intense activity. Additionally, during a run, skiers contract the large muscles of the leg, back, and abdomen for a relatively extended time before a brief rest during the turn transition, especially in long-radius turns. When the muscles are contracted, blood flow is diminished, which impedes lactate removal. Adapt your body to meet these anaerobic demands. Performance skiers should devote time to training at 80% to 90% of their maximum oxygen uptake.

Athletic Integration

Physiology and exercise are fascinating and complex subjects. Although much is known, there are still many questions. Trainers and coaches strive to devise better training programs. Even then, it is important for the individual to take charge of his development by learning more. In succeeding chapters, specific suggestions are provided for improving your athletic abilities. They will offer an approach that will lead you into skiing season at or near your top physical condition.

THREE

Fitness Testing

YOU PROBABLY KEEP a ledger of your finances, yet most recreational athletes don't think about recording how much they train or how much they get out of it. When it's sport as entertainment, there's really no need, but when you want to improve your physical condition, you ought to know if a program is working for you. Consider keeping a training log.

Simply enter each day's activities. You also should enter your resting heart rate each day, taken just after waking, and your weight each day. Sudden changes in these items are telltale indicators of overtraining. If your weight drops, your resting pulse rate increases, or your sleep patterns are disrupted, you should reduce your training loads. Also, set up a page where you can list dates and scores for the simple fitness test below.

MEDICAL CHECKUP. Before embarking on any fitness program, get a routine physical checkup. This is particularly important if you are over thirty-five. You should also have your cholesterol checked. The American Medical Association recommends a level below 200. With a clean bill of health, you are ready to start.

A stress test is usually recommended for people over fifty if you plan to use many of the strenuous anaerobic training routines. If you are from thirty-five to fifty, you may want to consider taking one, particularly if you or your family has a history of heart problems, diabetes, high blood pressure, or obesity, or if you smoke.

A stress test takes about thirty minutes, during which the cardiologist will closely monitor your heart during rigorous exercise. It is usually done on a treadmill that begins at slow speed, but the speed and slope increase so that by the end of the test, you are near your maximum heart rate. As you exercise, an electrocardiogram (EKG) is taken and your blood pressure is monitored. The EKG can show fifteen to twenty types of responses; essentially, the test shows if there is decreased blood flow to the heart muscle.

James Fixx, perhaps the man most responsible for popularizing running, died of a massive heart attack. It was said that a stress test could have detected his condition—had he bothered to take one.

TESTING FREQUENCY. Though a good conditioning program should yield rapid gains, they are not so fast that you may note specific improvements from week to week. By keeping a log and periodically taking short tests, you can quickly determine where you are physically throughout the year.

There are many tests in sports that rank you according to norms for your age. That is not the intent here.

The commonly used Wells Bend and Reach Test measures the flexibility of hamstrings and lower back muscles. While keeping his knees straight, the athlete pushes a small sliding tab beyond his feet.

The idea is for you to measure improvement only according to your own performance, so any activity in which you can standardize distance, time, and number of cycles or repetitions can be used, though you will find here tests that are fairly specific to skiing. You should space these tests out far enough so your body has time to adapt. If you refer to the periodization program in Chapter Eight, you will note the year is divided into five cycles: active rest, preparation, maximum strength, conversion, and maintenance. If you apply this schedule to your conditioning, test yourself at the beginning of the preparation cycle, at the end of the maximum strength cycle and after the conversion cycle, just before skiing begins. You may also want to test at the end of the skiing season to see where you've made gains or losses.

U.S. Ski Team Physical Fitness Medals Test

With the permission of the U.S. Ski Team, its Medals Test is reprinted below. It is easy to conduct but very hard to perform. All you need is a stopwatch, measured track, and a few friends with whom to do it.

This test was designed by Dr. Topper Hagerman and the U.S. Ski Team Sports Medicine Council for young athletes participating in U.S.S.A.-sanctioned alpine competitions. It is organized with age group standards for men and women.

Though this test evaluates fitness very specific to skiing, it is similar to tests performed on college football teams. It puts a premium on strength, power, and agility. Unfortunately, there are no standards for adults beyond the age of twenty-four. There is no reason why the committed older recreational athlete could not exceed these standards with some serious training.

Make no mistake: this is a rigorous test, and you may need to practice some of the exercise techniques for a good score. Doing all the tests at once would make for a strenuous workout. Nevertheless, among five active men between the ages of thirty-four and forty-one with whom I trained, at least one Seniors standard was achieved by everyone in the group at the start of fall training. Two months later, almost all standards were achieved by everyone.

As long as you do your best, don't get discouraged if

you don't make the standard. To get a better feel for where you stand, tally your result as a percentage of the standard. For instance, if you were a thirty-year-old man and ran the 440 in sixty-four seconds, you would divide the standard time of sixty multiplied by 100 by the time run to get 93.75%. As you train, you want to decrease this time by 7% before taking the test again. When you do, you can compare percentages from the first test with the last to gauge improvement over time.

DESCRIPTION OF TESTS. 40-yard dash. This requires speed and explosive leg power and is a measure of anaerobic fitness.

440-yard dash. The 440 is 80% to 90% anaerobic and 10% to 20% aerobic.

Mile run. Although the mile tests aerobic capability, it has a strong anaerobic factor near the finish. It is 60% to 70% aerobic and 30% to 40% anaerobic.

Jump and reach. This is a standard test to gauge leg power. It calls for a blackened plywood board five feet long and a foot wide. The board is marked in half-inch increments and should be mounted six inches from the wall. Use chalk on the fingertips to measure distance. Stand facing the wall, reach up, and touch to get a standing reach. Stand sideways to the board, jump, and touch to get a maximum jump mark. Mea-

Female members of the U.S. Ski Team perform some demanding bench jumps.

Event	Women (Ages)			
	12–13	14–15	16–18	19 +
40-yard dash	6.9 seconds	6.3 seconds	5.8 seconds	5.6 seconds
440-yard dash	78 seconds	72 seconds	71 seconds	70 seconds
1-mile run	7 minutes	6:45 minutes	6:10 minutes	6 minutes
Vertical jump	17 inches	18 inches	19 inches	20 inches
Bench jump	75	90	95	105
Push-ups	25	40	43	46
Sit-ups	45	52	54	58
Shuttle run	10 seconds	9.7 seconds	9.3 seconds	9 seconds

Event	Men (Ages)			
	12–13	14–15	16–18	19 +
40-yard dash	6 seconds	5.5 seconds	5.2 seconds	5 seconds
440-yard dash	70 seconds	65 seconds	64 seconds	60 seconds
1-mile run	6:35 minutes	5:55 minutes	5:35 minutes	5:25 minutes
Vertical jump	18 inches	23 inches	24 inches	25 inches
Bench jump	80	95	100	115
Push-ups	30	50	55	60
Sit-ups	48	53	55	60
Shuttle run	9.8 seconds	9.2 seconds	8.9 seconds	8.5 seconds

sure the distance. Record the highest of three jumps. You can also repeat facing the opposite direction.

Bench jumps. This tests muscular strength, power, endurance, coordination, and agility. String a rope just slightly higher than the kneecap. Have somebody hold at least one end so that if the athlete jumps short, the rope can be released and he won't fall. Jump back and forth over the rope. Over and back counts as two jumps. Do as many as possible in sixty seconds.

Push-ups. This is a good indicator of upper-body strength. There is no time limit, but you must do all push-ups continuously. Assume the position of front-leaning rest. Touch your chest to the floor on each push-up while keeping your back and legs straight.

Sit-ups. This is a test of abdominal and hip flexor strength. Lie flat on your back with hands clasped behind your head and knees bent. Have someone hold your feet down. Do as many as possible in sixty seconds.

Shuttle run. This is a challenging test to determine speed and agility. Start from a standing position behind one of two lines thirty feet apart. Behind the other line are two two-by-two-by-four-inch blocks of wood. At the signal, run to the line, pick up one block, and run back. Place, don't drop, the block on the ground behind the starting line. Run back and get the other block, turn around, and cross the starting line holding the second block. Score the best of two attempts.

Additional Testing

Once you've logged your results from the Medals Test, you're done until next time. If you want more, here are additional things you can do to gauge your skiing fitness.

VERTICAL JUMP POWER TESTING. Athletes don't train for fitness; they train for performance. What determines performance in a sport like skiing is not absolute strength or power, but strength and power relative to body weight.

The vertical jump is an excellent test of leg power, combining strength and speed of muscle contraction. If you have a vertical jump of twenty inches and you weigh 170 pounds, you produce more power than a friend who jumps just as high but weighs 160 pounds.

In the Medals Test, the vertical jump test norms do not take body weight into account. This is okay for racers because gates on a course are the same distance apart for all competitors, so there is a minimum distance everyone has to cover regardless of their mass.

If you do a lot of strength conditioning, you will get stronger, but if your vertical jump does not improve much, it may be because you gained ten pounds of muscle. To fairly record changes in your power output, even if your weight changes, use this method:

1. Determine your vertical jump in meters (multiply inches by 0.0254).

2. Find the square root of this distance.

3. Multiply the result of step two by your weight in pounds (kilograms multiplied by 2.21).

For example, a 180-pound athlete has a vertical jump of twenty-four inches:

1. $24 \times 0.0254 = 0.6096$

2. Square root $= 0.781$

3. $0.781 \times 180 = 140.58$

For a comparison with a world-class athlete, football player Herschel Walker recorded a standing vertical

The Vertec measures an athlete's vertical jump, an accurate indicator of leg power. The individual bats to one side the highest tabs he can reach.

jump of 40.5 inches at a weight of 222 pounds. His power output was 225.2.

Once you figure your power quotient, you can compare it to these guidelines developed at Ohio State University. Don't take the standards too seriously, as they were developed for another closely measured power test and the correlations tend to vary. This jump test is easier to conduct, however.

Incidentally, you can see what kind of a horse you are by multiplying your score by 0.013 to derive horse-

Power Quotient Guidelines

	Men (Ages)				
Rating	**15–20**	**20–30**	**30–40**	**40–50**	**50 +**
Poor	<113	<106	<85	<65	<50
Fair	113–149	106–139	85–111	65–84	50–65
Average	150–187	140–175	112–140	85–105	66–82
Good	188–224	176–210	141–168	106–125	83–98
Excellent	224>	210>	168>	125>	98>

	Women (Ages)				
Rating	**15–20**	**20–30**	**30–40**	**40–50**	**50 +**
Poor	<92	<85	<65	<50	<38
Fair	92–120	85–111	65–84	50–65	38–48
Average	121–151	112–140	85–105	66–82	49–61
Good	152–182	141–168	106–125	83–98	62–75
Excellent	182>	168>	125>	98>	75>

power. In the case of our 180-pound athlete, he is producing 1.828 horsepower. Herschel Walker's result indicates 2.928 horsepower.

Without referring to other guidelines, you can determine your power output with two other tests. In addition to the vertical jump, measure leg power with standing broad jumps performed facing forward, then backward, and facing sideways on both sides. You can also do a short sprint test. Time a fifty-yard dash that begins with a fifteen-yard running head start so you

Members of the Breckenridge, Colorado, Ski Team use horizontal jumps during summer training to evaluate their power.

are at full speed as you cross the starting line. Multiply your weight by the distance and divide the product by the elapsed time. Log the result for comparison later in the conditioning cycle.

TRAINING HEART RATE. Throughout any workout, you should periodically monitor your pulse. The sprints, relays, and minute drills will elevate your pulse frequently to its maximum rate, which you will quickly determine. More important is that it will not take you long to also determine how quickly your pulse settles down to where you are ready for a repeat. Many athletes use heart rate monitors. It's cheaper to place your fingers over your carotid artery in the neck, count the beats for six seconds, and multiply by ten.

During a workout, your pulse will rise for two or three minutes to develop the anaerobic capacity and power needed for performance skiing. By closely monitoring your pulse at rest, you can maintain it close to the level indicated for aerobic conditioning throughout the session.

Your maximum heart rate can be determined from a stress test, or you can estimate it by subtracting your age from 220, though this may deviate by plus or minus ten beats per minute.

To determine your training heart rate, you also want to know your resting heart rate. Monitor your pulse for one minute in the morning, immediately after waking up. Then do these steps:

1. Subtract your resting heart rate from your maximum heart rate.

2. Multiply the remainder by 0.7.

3. Add the resting pulse to the product of step two.

For example, for a thirty-year-old athlete with a waking heart rate of 48:

1. $220 - 30 = 190$ (maximum heart rate)
2. $190 - 48 = 142$ (adjusted heart rate)
3. $142 \times 0.7 = 99.4$
4. $99.4 + 48 = 147.4$ (training heart rate)

The aerobic training effect occurs when the heart is elevated to 60% of its maximum rate for twenty minutes or more, though the formula above indicates using 0.7 as a multiplier. If you are starting out and need some time to adapt to greater intensities or are conditioning aerobically with distance running or

As an athlete's heart rate increases, so does his oxygen uptake (VO₂ Maximum), though not in direct proportion.

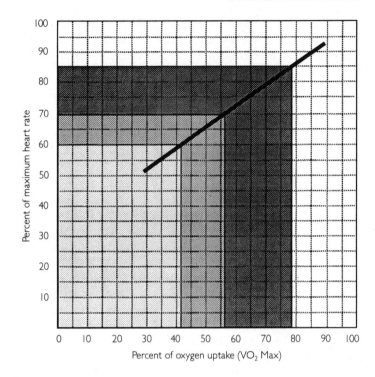

cycling during the active rest or preparation cycles discussed in Chapter Eight, use 0.6 as a multiplier in step three. To determine your training pulse rate for high-intensity track intervals or minute drills, use 0.75 up to 0.9 as a multiplier.

OXYGEN UPTAKE. For the recreational athlete, pulse rates are all that are needed to determine good training and exertion levels. More precise testing, however, is needed to determine your oxygen uptake, expressed as liters of oxygen consumed per minute.

There is a correlation between your heart rate and how much oxygen you consume, though oxygen uptake is more relative to the heart rate as exertion increases. The correlation varies depending on what exercises are performed, so elite athletes can adjust their training if they gauge their exercise intensities as percentages of their oxygen uptake. Only the A team of the U.S. Ski Team is given this test; B and C team members are evaluated with the Medals Test.

The test is performed on a treadmill or bicycle ergometer. Like the stress test, the work load progressively increases. During the test, exhaled gases are collected for analysis. The point where the athlete can no longer increase his oxygen consumption despite increased work load is the maximum oxygen uptake, or VO$_2$ Max.

ANAEROBIC CAPACITY. Unlike aerobic endurance, anaerobic power is difficult to assess because total energy output cannot be accurately measured at high levels.

The Wingate test, though it does not exhaust the athlete's anaerobic capacity, measures maximum out-

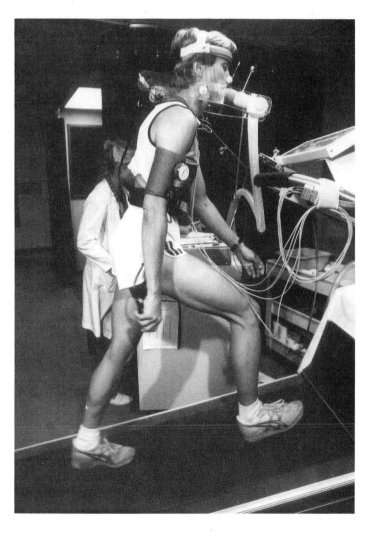

To determine her oxygen uptake, former Nordic U.S. Ski Team member Pat Engberg exhales into a gas-collecting apparatus while walking on a treadmill that gradually increases in speed and pitch.

put and its drop-off over a thirty- or sixty-second period. This test is performed on a bicycle ergometer. The tension is set relative to body weight. After sufficient warm-up, the athlete sprints for sixty seconds. A monitor counts the revolutions and the number recorded at every five-second mark. The results show maximum power, average power, and the drop-off in high-intensity endurance.

BODY COMPOSITION. Proper nutrition and a high strength-to-weight ratio are important to performance skiers. Excess body fat is an extra suitcase to carry. For most skiers, being quick and strong, getting into last season's pants, and simply feeling comfortable in

At the University of Utah's PEAK Academy, downhiller Jeff Olson cranks out the final few seconds of a Wingate test. Results from this exhausting test give a good indication of the athlete's anaerobic capacity.

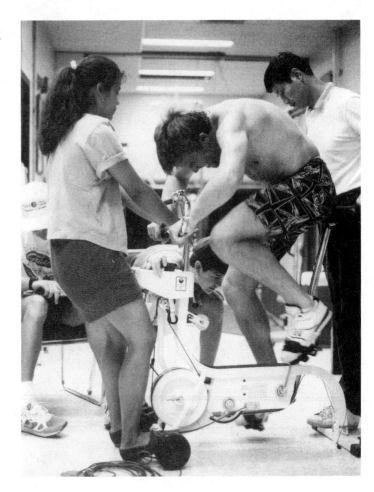

A Breckenridge Ski Team member checks her fitness. She is timed as she works her way around the apparatus three times, jumping over each bar. This simple test helps her gauge her progress and provides an excellent workout.

their own skin is all that's important. Most elite skiers don't have the lean, ectomorphic shape of the marathon runner. Extremely low percentages of body fat among skiers can also be a cold-weather disadvantage.

Though the AMA has recently revised its height and weight charts upward, particularly for older people, these figures are often out of whack for athletes who train often with weights. The best way to determine your optimum body composition is with underwater weighing or a skin-fold test. Underwater weighing is the most accurate, but the skin-fold test is very close. Other methods are common but can be unreliable.

The skin-fold test measures subcutaneous fat, which constitutes about half of body fat, with calipers at different locations. Underwater weighing works on the principle that fat floats and everything else sinks. After determining your dry weight, it is easy to calculate your lean body mass. These tests can be very helpful if you feel you need to lose or gain some weight.

Oxygen uptake, Wingate, and body composition tests are unnecessary for the great majority of skiers, though if you are interested, contact a good sports medicine clinic or a local university where they may be conducted.

FOUR

Flexibility

THINK ABOUT a typical skier off for a weekend trip. He wakes up at 5:30 A.M., downs several cups of coffee, and sits with his knees stuck into his chest for the two-hour trip. He straps heavy skis and boots to his feet, then takes a cold chair ride to the summit. Then he blasts down the mountain with his hair on fire. What's wrong with this picture? This same person wouldn't go out of the house on a warm afternoon for a twenty-minute jog without first stretching out the muscles.

Skiers ignore stretching for a couple of reasons. They are too eager once they've hit the top of the mountain, particularly when there's new powder. Because many stretches are done seated or lying down, no one wants to flop down in the snow. Many people don't consider stretching important because they ski in a fairly compact position without twisting much.

It is important to stretch immediately before skiing and to stay flexible in general throughout the year. It's worth repeating that muscles that are stretched and warmed up will contract faster and more fully than cold, unstretched muscles. Unlike most of the other elements of physical fitness, flexibility will not improve by just skiing. Regular stretching, though, can produce impressive gains after only a month or two.

You don't need to make a big production out of stretching. Here are a few exercises you can do without taking off your skis:

Think about a few upper-body stretches while riding the chair. Roll your head around and use a hand to pull or push your head down in front, back, and side to side. Stretch your arms and shoulders by pulling one arm across your chest with the other. Stretch your wrists by holding your left hand palm down in front of your chest and using the right hand over your knuckles to push the back of your hand down and toward your elbow. Now turn both hands palm up in front of your chest. Place the fingers of your right hand around your left thumb, and center your right thumb on the ridge of your left hand just below the little finger. Hold your left arm in close to your body and push it down gently. Your wrist will get a strong outward twisting stretch.

Lace your fingers together with thumbs up, then rotate your wrists 180 degrees so they are pointing down, then straighten your elbows.

At the summit, ski off to a flat spot to stretch for a few minutes. Do some groin stretches by widely separating your skis and leaning out over one knee. Stretch your hamstring by raising a leg and propping the tail of your ski into the snow, then try to touch your raised knee with your head. Bring one leg behind you and stuff the ski tip in the snow while balancing with your poles. Stretch your quadriceps by flexing your other knee.

Separate your feet and point your ski tips apart. Plant your poles behind you with your hands still in the grips. Squat down so your knees are bent more than ninety degrees. Take both poles and place them in the snow away to one side. Holding the grips, lean the same-side hip into the snow as if you were severely angulated. Hold the poles horizontally in front at both the grips and above the basket. Now try to raise your arms straight over your head and back behind you. This will give you a good chest and shoulder stretch.

When you take your first run, ease into it. Your car needs to be driven slowly until it warms up to operating temperature; so do your muscles and cardio-

On the Hill

respiratory system. I always ski better and harder throughout the day if I take the first run or two by myself, usually on easier slopes. Besides warming up, I tune in to my own sense of coordination and vitality without the distraction of playing catch-up to some other ridge runner.

Throughout the day, you will tighten up, so do a little more stretching as you go along. Taking care not to bonk anyone else in the lift line with your ski, do a hamstring or groin stretch. When you take a breather, plant both poles uphill and put your hip into the hill to stretch your sides.

Stretching Routines for Life

FREESTYLE STRETCHING. Most people think of stretching as something to do just before working out. It takes a lot of discipline to go through a twice-daily ten-minute stretching routine, but that is the best recommendation. You can stretch during other normal daily activities. For instance, read the evening newspaper seated on the floor with your feet together and your knees pulled up to the side. When you're tired of this, stand up, spread your legs, and continue to read the paper on the floor. How about washing dishes with one leg up on the counter for thirty seconds at a time? You could do a half-dozen stretches on the floor while talking to someone on the phone.

TOP-TO-BOTTOM STRETCHES. Stretching is not the same thing as warming up. Warm your muscles before stretching with a little light exercise like jogging, calisthenics, easy stationary cycling, or rowing. This elevates metabolism, lubricates joints, increases blood flow to the muscles, and raises their temperature. Stretching without a warm-up is like trying to chew cold bubble gum. Whenever you stretch, have a little routine in mind. Start at the top of your body and work down, or vice versa.

Here are some stretches that will address most of the major muscle groups. Use slow, steady movement. Hold positions from ten to thirty seconds, relax, then stretch again. At the limit of your flexibility, you should feel tightness, maybe even discomfort, but not pain. Obviously, if you have any joint problems, be cautious.

1. Rotate head front and back, side to side. Use a hand to push the head a little farther in each direction.

2. Raise your shoulders to your ears, then roll them back around in big circles; change directions. Give yourself a big hug with your elbows up high and one elbow over the top of your other forearm. Pull in with the outside arm. Reach overhead and behind you to touch between your shoulders. Place your other hand on your raised elbow and push down.

3. Reach behind you with both arms, one behind your head, the other behind your waist. Try to hook your fingers so you can pull them together.

4. Place one hand on a wall with your arm high and extended. Twist slowly away from the wall with your upper body.

5. Swing your arms in big, slow circles. Change direction.

6. Lie on your back and pull one knee into your chest with your arms. Pull both knees into your chest. Lie on your stomach and extend your back slightly by pushing up off the floor with your arms.

7. Spread your feet and place your hands on your hips. Slowly twist down and around in big circles. Change direction. Place your right hand on the hip and the left arm up over your head. Bend to the right

side as far as you can without breaking forward at the waist.

8. This is commonly known as "the pretzel." Sit on the floor with your right leg out in front. Cross your left leg over so the left foot rests on the floor by your thigh. Twist your upper body to the left and look over your left shoulder. Place your left hand on the ground behind you for balance, then hook your right elbow around your left thigh so it pushes in on your knee. The stretch comes from pushing the knee toward your midline with the elbow.

9. Sit on the floor. Straighten your right leg in front and bring your left foot up across your thigh. Reach under and around your left thigh and calf with both arms. Cradle the leg and pull it up into your chest.

10. Sit on the floor. Straighten a leg and place your other foot on your knee. Gently push down on the knee of your bent leg.

11. Sit on the floor, legs out in front. Touch your toes and try to hold your feet. Slowly straighten the legs. After stretching a bit, lower your head toward your thighs. Lie on your back and pull one knee to your chest. Lace your fingers together behind the foot. Straighten the leg and use your arms to raise your leg higher in the air.

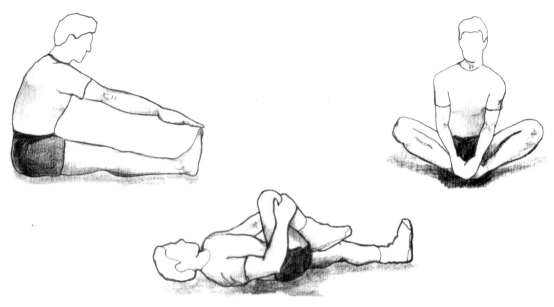

12. Spread your legs far apart, feet flat. Pivot ninety degrees in either direction. Slowly flex one knee so the other leg extends. Keep your back erect and chest up. Push the knee of your extended leg slowly toward the floor. You should feel a strong stretch in the groin and in the hamstrings of your extended leg.

13. From this position, in which your weight is forward over one knee, keep your hips low but straighten the bent knee and flex the knee of the straight leg, which will move your weight back over the rear knee. Again, try to keep your back erect and chest up.

14. Sit on the floor. Put the bottoms of your feet together and with your hands, pull them in toward your groin. Still holding your feet, press down lightly with your elbows.

15. The hurdler's stretch is well-known. Sit on the floor with one leg extended in front, the other behind with bent knee. Incline your upper body toward the straight knee. If you have bad knees, do the same exercise, but don't put your other leg behind you. Bend the knee but place your foot up high in your groin area.

16. Stand up, spread your legs far apart, and place your hands on the floor in front of you. Slowly walk back on your hands.

17. Do the hurdler's stretch. With one hand behind

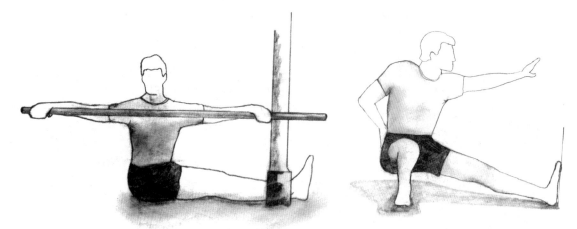

for balance, slowly arch your back, and lean back until your knee just comes up off the ground. You can stretch the hip a little by pushing it forward on the bent-knee side.

18. Sit on your knees with your toes inward. Place your hands well behind you and slowly lower your upper body back over your calves. Stop when your knees raise off the floor. Stand up, bring your foot up behind you, and hold onto your foot with the same-side hand. Balance on your other foot and bend forward at the waist. Now do the same stretch with the same leg, but switch hands.

Stretching is essential to any exercise program.

19. Lean against a wall with your arms straight, keeping your feet flat on the ground. Bend one knee to raise your heel and rock forward slowly in your hips.

20. Stand away from the wall and deeply flex your outside leg. Place the foot of your leg nearest the wall flat up against it. Keeping your balance, partially straighten your bent knee.

21. Sit on the floor and cross one leg over the other. Rotate your foot around in all directions with your hands. Walk around in a circle slowly with your ankles first inverted, then everted.

Two-Person Stretches

With a partner, you can stretch safely beyond what you could normally do by playing a little trick on your body. By alternately contracting and stretching a muscle, you engage what is known as the proprioceptive neuromuscular facilitation response, or PNF.

If you sit on the floor and try to touch your head to your knees abruptly, the muscles of your back and hamstrings will quickly contract to protect themselves from damage. On the other hand, if you slowly stretch forward and hold this position for ten seconds, then try to straighten up in the opposite direction for a few seconds while your partner provides resistance, you should be able to relax and stretch farther forward than on your first attempt. Proper PNF stretching is a good way to really push your muscles and joints to their limit. Be sure your partner applies resistance only as far as is reasonably comfortable to you. He can help you maintain a good stretched position after the resistance phase, but this must be even.

Here are two other partner-PNF stretches. Given these examples, you can develop other stretches that use the same principles:

Shoulders. Have your partner pull your hands slowly together up high and behind your back. Stretch passively for ten seconds, then, as your partner provides resistance, try to bring your arms forward for three to five seconds. Relax and again allow the arms to stretch passively back.

Hamstrings and lower back. Lie on your back and raise one of your legs straight up. Have your partner push it back toward your chest. Stretch slowly and carefully for ten seconds. Now contract the stretched muscles by trying to lower your leg for three to five seconds, then relax again and allow your partner to slowly stretch your leg back again.

Lower back. You don't always have to use a partner to get this effect. This stretch is used by kayakers to loosen the lower back. Sit on the floor with legs extended in front. Place both feet against one side of a solid upright beam. Hold the end of a bar or broomstick (or kayak paddle) with both hands about shoulder width apart. Place the forward end of the bar on the opposite side of the beam. Push slowly out with a straight rear arm and pull in with the forward arm for ten seconds. Resist the movement by tightening your back muscles for three to five seconds, then relax and slowly stretch again. Be careful, as you can apply a lot of leverage to your lower back with the bar.

Relaxation

Being a fun-loving lot, most skiers don't have trouble relaxing. In conditioning for skiing, there are mental and physical relaxations.

BODY RELAXATION. There are two sides to physical conditioning: hard training, then recovery and restoration. To improve, you must consolidate the gains from training by allowing your body to regenerate. You need liquids, food, sleep, and time for your muscle fibers to repair themselves.

Immediately after a strenuous workout, your body is tense. Many athletes have trouble sleeping if they work out late in the evening. You should always stretch out

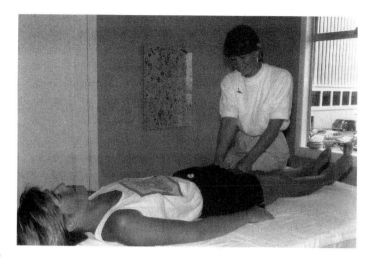

Massage during the recovery phase encourages flexibility, reduces stress, and relaxes. Deep-tissue massage improves posture and body alignment.

to reduce muscle tightness, but before showering and fixing dinner, give your muscles a total break as a little reward.

Lie on your back on the floor and close your eyes. Isometrically contract the muscles of your body for a few seconds, then relax deeply. Concentrate on your breathing. Slowly work from your toes up, completely relaxing the muscles of your feet, calves, thighs, hamstrings, and buttocks, right to the top of your head, down your arms, and out your fingers. This takes some mental effort; you can't just go to sleep. Imagine your body is a balloon, and the helium is slowly leaking out of it as you settle to the floor. Or, imagine your limbs slowly turning to lead. By concentrating on relaxing each little muscle group, you will often find that after a moment or two, part of your body abruptly goes limp, even though you were sure it was relaxed when you started. In this case, you've allowed the muscle to relax beyond its normal resting state.

Most larger skiing areas have swimming pools or hot tubs, which can be godsends for aching muscles. Massages are nice and stimulate blood flow, which may help reduce lactic acid buildup. Self-massage is cheaper and easy, using firm kneading pressure on your thighs and calves.

Short of chiropractic manipulation, if you are really looking for the ultimate massage, consider getting rolfed. Named for its developer, Ida Rolf, rolfing is a form of deep-tissue massage and manipulation that realigns your body structure over ten sessions. It can be intense but has an undeserved reputation for being painful. Most people don't recognize that through use and abuse, some muscles become dominant, causing posture misalignment. One shoulder or hip may be slightly higher than the other, one foot is splayed out while the other is straight, or the head is chronically canted forward, causing the shoulder muscles to constantly contract to support it. These can add up to chronic back pain, headaches, fatigue, and stress. Through rolfing, these imbalances can be equalized and you can learn how to retain this new symmetry. Skiers gain a more efficient structure that can withstand greater loads.

MENTAL RELAXATION. The mental aspect of performance skiing appears contradictory. On the one hand, you must concentrate and pay attention. On the other, you must let your neuromuscular autopilot take over. By admonishing yourself to concentrate or think, you simply confuse matters.

Learning to channel your feelings when day-to-day anxiety sets in can help avert nervous reactions during critical times while skiing. If you can't go with the flow when speeds increase or the slope gets steep, you're in deep trouble.

Anxiety is difficult to wish away, but you can override it. Get back to the basics. Focus on the most important thing in your life—breathing. Close your eyes and feel the air flowing in and out. Imagine your lungs rising and falling like a bellows. Do this often enough and you should be able to relieve anxiety with only a moment of meditation.

Some days, you feel at the top of your game. Other days, nothing seems to go right. This will always be the case, but at the upper level of any sport, attitude counts for more than talent. If you get down on yourself, it only gets harder to pull out of the basement.

Perhaps you need a few runs off by yourself where you can focus on your senses. Listen to your skis. Do they make a clean, sharp sound, or do they sound like a snow shovel scraping along the walk? Can you feel the snow under your boots? Are your toes curled up, or can you wiggle them? Can you feel the tip of the ski bend as you enter a turn? Where are your hands? Where are you looking? These kinds of questions can help get you more in tune with your surroundings.

If you could get all the same thrills while skiing in an indoor stadium, would you be as committed to it? One reason skiing is so great is because of the beautiful mountain scenery. But when you ski the same area all the time, it's easy to take it for granted. Instead of blasting down every run trying to stay up with your buddies, smell the evergreens once in a while. It's another way to tamp down the mental chatter and let your skis do their job.

FIVE

Boot Camp for Snow Warriors

FALL IS the most fabulous time of year, full of anticipation for another ski season. The weather becomes cool, windy, and rainy, and weekend football games and jogs through falling leaves celebrate a time when energy runs high.

For many serious skiers, fall is the time to head to playing fields and gymnasiums for the annual ritual known as dryland conditioning. Weight training and running are good, but power, agility, and coordination are developed through the dryland workout. From September through November, workouts specific to skiing are conducted two, three, or four days per week. It's a lot of work, but you also can make it fun.

A dryland program should keep your interest by posing different challenges. Exercises can often be thought of as games. You can change the rules or create variations as you go, which keeps you a little off balance, but within weeks, you will notice a new vigor in your attitude, quickness of movement, and an appetite for a little mud and sweat. The intensity can be high, so if you feel something strain or pull, back off!

Getting Organized

PARTNERS. Exercising by yourself is hard. There are no excuses for not finding a group. Almost all ski teams conduct dryland training. Many YMCAs, YWCAs, health clubs, aerobics studios, and universities offer ski conditioning. Or, phone some skiing buddies and arrange for regular get-togethers after school or work. Partners encourage and push you to do your best. Dryland training, though, shouldn't be overly competitive. Incorporate some relay races, ultimate Frisbee, or three-on-a-side basketball, but don't let the competition get out of hand. Try to challenge yourself inwardly.

LEADING A GROUP. Skip this section if you're working out by yourself or with one or two others. It may be particularly helpful to instructors or coaches.

If you're not working out in an organized group and there are more than three people, select a leader for each session. Trade the role around for a little variety. The leader should keep the workout moving while allowing for sufficient rest between exercises. In particular, the leader should offer encouragement.

If you plan a difficult, high-intensity workout, get everyone on your side. Evaluate the condition of the group. With widely diverging abilities, have two or three subgroups with different goals. Have a motivating rally. Conditioning coaches for the U.S. Ski Team have athletes choose a word for the day in a huddle and yell, "What's the word?" when the going gets tough.

The larger the group, the more important is the leader's role. The most frustrating workouts are the ones in which people mill around. Organizing multiteam, multitask relays can be a nightmare without a plan. Here are some examples of effective group management:

A group of twenty is ready to start with stretching, followed by some relay races. You, the leader, announce, "Follow me!" and take off running. Once on the field, you run in a large circle. When everyone is in the circle and the size looks good, you call, "Stop!" and take a position in the middle. For a larger circle, everyone takes one step back; for a smaller one, one step forward. Spread people out by having them touch fingertip to fingertip. If you need paired partners, the leader can have the group count off, quickly going around the circle. Don't just say, "Grab a partner," because you're guaranteed to have some strays. If the group is extra large, you might want two concentric circles, in which case you can have the Number Ones take a step forward and the Twos a step back. To create two teams evenly matched with men and women, first have only the women count by twos, then the men. To form lines, escort a leadoff person to a position and ask all others with that number to line up alongside or behind him. Again, spread people out by having them touch fingertips.

The point is that too much explanation only confuses people. You can orchestrate anything with simple, one-at-a-time instructions.

MORE IS SORE. Even if your summer was full of strenuous activity, limit your fall workouts at first. Efficient dryland programs can take as little as sixty to ninety minutes. Even if you are fit, expect soreness when you begin a program specific to skiing. Your body will let you know quickly if you are pushing too hard.

For a long time, muscle soreness from exercise was attributed to lactic acid buildup, but the creaky stiffness and weakness you feel eight to twenty-four hours after a hard session is more apt to be caused by microtears in the muscle fibers and tendons, plus some fluid buildup. Time is the only real healer and will result in stronger muscles than before. You can help alleviate the symptoms by gradually increasing your intensity and then through stretching before and after exercise, drinking fluids, massage, whirlpool therapy, and by taking aspirin or ibuprofen.

LOCATION. Find a good place to work out. The ideal location would be a lighted football field with a 440-yard track next to an indoor basketball court and par course, with lots of nearby hills, stairs, and trails to run.

If you are part of a group, maybe you can persuade school or park administrators to let you use their gyms. Useful accessories include cones, Hula Hoops, basketballs, jump ropes, low benches, and a few bamboo poles. Most important is a stopwatch.

Warm-Up and Progression

For maximum effect, routines should become progressively intense, then conclude with cool-down stretching.

JOG AND STRETCH. Start every workout by warming up the muscles and shifting your system into a little higher gear. If you're at a track, an easy two or three times around should make you break a sweat. Never forget the warm-up.

Next, stretch your muscles. Without a good stretch, quick movements can cause stress injuries to muscles or joints. To ensure you get all the muscles, start your stretching from the head and work your way down. Do each stretch slowly, without bouncing, for twenty seconds. Relax and repeat.

PROGRESSION. Stretching can work right into some of the lighter calisthenics. For instance, lunge walking can really work your quadriceps and buttocks, and stretches the groin. You might prefer some agility drills at this point, with some tree slaloms, ball drills, or runs through a par course.

Save the more exhausting leg routines for the end of your session to help build endurance. Sometimes it's fun to really exhaust the legs and back with strength routines, then try some agility drills to see how well you can respond. However, this can be counterproductive, since you can't develop complex motor skills without a fresh set of legs. Consider an occasional day when you might emphasize quickness, balance, and coordination, and another when you just hammer the legs with strength and endurance exercises.

PULSATE. In a group, take pulses after each exercise. Have the person with a stopwatch call out, "Pulse, ready, count!" Everyone else places their fingers at the carotid artery and counts until the monitor shouts "Stop!" at six seconds. By doing this frequently, you will soon get a good feeling for how intensely and efficiently you can work over short periods. You will also discover how quickly you recover and at what pulse rate you are best prepared to go at it again.

Running and Track Work

Besides being fun, summer distance running builds aerobic endurance and conditions the muscles, ligaments, and tendons for high-intensity work. In the fall, it's time to change gears.

THE NEED FOR SPEED. Runners who want to move faster know they must vary their training. Long, slow distance running only makes you efficient at running long distances slowly because it tends to work

Former U.S. Ski Team member Carolyn Curl adds some variety to her afternoon run. First, she darts between posts . . .

. . . then she gets some air time by leaping over them. Such impromptu activities can be incorporated into any workout.

primarily slow-twitch muscle fibers; running faster means recruiting the fast-twitch fibers. For performance skiers, speed work develops strong legs for powerful leaps, jumps, and bounds.

The easiest way to get into speed work is through *fartlek* training, which is Swedish for speed play. The idea is to vary your running with pace, speed, or time. Accelerate from your normal pace and run at faster paces at random points during a distance run.

Intervals involve more structured distances, ranging from forty yards to a mile. Given the length of a ski run, a particularly good distance is the 440. This is a tough race because it is short enough to make you push yourself at nearly full speed but long enough to completely test your stamina.

Sixty seconds of hard running may not seem like a lot, but you'll soon see how tough it is. It is best done with friends who will push one another and in moderate doses to avoid injury. Because you get to rest between bouts on the track, your total energy expenditure in four 440s will be considerably greater than what you could expend in a one-mile run.

HILLS AND DALES. Related to speed work is hill running and bounding. Hill running is especially good for your legs and buttocks, as you have to lift yourself from a partial squat.

Too much hill running can soon lead to injury. Pushing off of your toes on a grade hyperextends the Achilles tendon and small muscle tendons on the outside lower leg. If you notice irritation or low-grade pain in these areas, back off.

What goes up must come down, and downhill running puts an eccentric load on the quadriceps and stresses the knees. You are better off pushing hard up hills, then walking, traversing, or slow jogging back down. When you're running short hills, pair with someone of your own approximate height and weight, and carry him on your back up the hill. It's not a good idea to do so going back down, however.

STAIRS. Most ski racers have run stadium stairs because it develops great leg extension strength, and since each step is flat, you hyperextend the lower leg tendons much less.

Vary your stair running by running every step, every other step, or hopping up a flight with feet together. Walk down stairs for safety's sake and to rest for the next flight. If there's a large group in a stadium, run one flight and then walk over one flight before going down, to keep from getting in the way of those running up. Spread out so if one person trips, he won't take out everyone else domino-style.

Plyometrics

Plyometric exercises were developed by trainers in the Eastern bloc countries to condition fast-twitch muscles to respond quickly and powerfully. Because it stresses muscles so much, plyometric training should follow conventional strength training.

A basic plyometric exercise involves fast prestretch-ing of a muscle, followed by an equally quick contrac-tion of the muscle. For instance, if you jump off of a low bench and land on your toes, with very little flex-ing of your knees, you can rebound off of your toes powerfully.

There are a number of plyometric exercises suited for skiers, such as jumping from a low bench, then rebounding off the floor to land on the bench again. Other exercises include lateral jumps over a low bench or rope; repeated tuck jumps; lunge jumping; hop, skip, and jump; and running with long, leaping bounds.

You may recognize some of the exercises without ever having heard the word "plyometrics." When doing these, try to get explosive movement going as soon as you've applied the prestretch, and make sure you don't overdo it too soon.

Minute Drills

Minute drills are timed exercises with cyclical move-ments, as is skiing. They don't have to last a minute. When you're just starting out, try thirty seconds. When you're experienced, try two to five minutes, depending on the exercise. Minute drills develop strength, but because you are using body weight only, they emphasize power and muscle endurance.

There are dozens of these exercises for skiers. These really put the skiing muscles to work:

CONE DRILLS. The fluorescent cones used for soc-cer training are great for slalom and obstacle courses for skiers. If you don't have cones, borrow all your part-ners' extra shoes. In cone drills, there is a lot of room for imagination.

Slalom. For starters, set a short offset slalom and time each run. Run or hop forward, backward, on one foot or two. Tuck jump down and back. Run around each cone and touch your outside hand to the ground at each one by flexing deeply in the knees. Emphasize skiing form by keeping both feet six inches apart and your inside foot slightly ahead. Vary this exercise by touching your inside hand to the ground at each cone. Speed is important, but so is control. If you get out of balance or start knocking over cones, slow down and perfect your technique.

Box courses. Timed box courses can be challenging. On one-half of a regulation basketball court, imagine eight stations along the boundary lines: one in each corner, one on each sideline at midcourt, and one at each endline in the middle. Like numbers on a clock, the stations are at twelve, one, three, five, six, seven, nine, and eleven. The runner starts at center court and on "go," sprints forward to twelve, runs backward to center; runs forward to one, backward to center; sideways to three, sideways to center; backward to five, forward to center, and so forth, all the way around, to finish at center court.

Control is critical for speed, since you can lose a half-second at each station by overstepping or understepping. You'll learn some interesting things about technique. If you can touch all eight stations and get back to center eight times in forty seconds or less, you can consider yourself a total animal, though I have seen a thirteen-year-old junior girl run a full circuit in forty-two seconds. Try running the same pattern with much shortened three-step distances for another variation.

Box race course. Add a little one-on-one competition with a timed box race course. You can have a sixty-five-yard parallel course with two 180-degree and two 90-degree direction changes, and no risk of athletes running into one another. The trick is to stag-

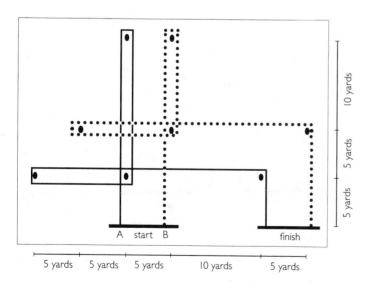

5 yards   5 yards   5 yards   10 yards   5 yards

A   start   B   finish

10 yards

5 yards

5 yards

A box racecourse can add stimulating competition to your training. When the parallel courses are set up properly, there is little chance that athletes A and B will collide.

ger the cones so that each athlete runs an equal distance once, then runs five yards longer and five yards shorter, twice.

If you stage a race, pair athletes of equal ability. Matched runners would round turns one, three, and the finish at the same time, but where paths intersect at turns two and four, there are five-yard differentials that should keep runners from colliding.

By using the corner of a football field, the yard markers will give you the distance to the first turn and make the third turnaround point for both courses flush with the sideline. You can probably come up with some clever variations.

Stay loose in the shoes. You can look pretty sharp running cone drills indoors wearing court shoes or on grass in soccer cleats, but with ordinary tennis shoes, your feet will slide. Also, to change direction, you need better balance to compensate for less traction.

LUNGE WALKING. Place your hands on your hips or behind your head and take a long step forward. Lower the knee of your rear leg so it's close to touching the ground. Be careful not to drop the knee too fast or you'll smash it. Now extend up on the forward leg, pull the rear leg through, and repeat.

Start slowly, then try a tougher variation by jumping off the forward leg and switching legs while both feet are in the air. After twenty yards of this exercise, you will have many new feelings in your legs.

Done forward or backward, the lunge walk and lunge jump are excellent exercises for developing leg strength and power.

Girardellis are among the best exercises to develop quickness and endurance for skiing.

GIRARDELLIS. Supposedly, when asked about the best exercise for skiing, Marc Girardelli demonstrated the reaction drill that made him such a champion, so it was named after him. Besides having such a motivating name, this exercise is also highly specific.

Place two parallel lines of cones anywhere from ten feet to thirty-six feet apart. Stand between the lines. At "go," run back and forth between them. As you come to a line, face in the same direction as that line and touch the ground with your outside hand. Do this by bending the knees rather than at the waist. Sometimes set the lines far enough apart to get up to full running speed before having to slow down for the turn. At other times, set the distance for just a bound or two.

A mini-Girardelli can be done with no running. Flex your right knee and touch the ground with your right hand as you cross the left leg behind you, then extend laterally to the left to switch sides. Once you have the rhythm going, try it with the leg crossing in front of you. This will really make you feel like you are countering on your skis. Now do minis both ways but with a jump in the air to switch sides.

BENCH JUMPING. This classic skiing exercise particularly favors a high strength-to-weight ratio. Don't select a bench too high or massive, in case you tangle your feet. Actually, a rope tied to a post and held by a partner is safer than a bench and helps develop bounding skills. Hold the rope just above knee high. Partners on their knees can make a wonderful short bench.

A simple bench jump would be done laterally, keeping the arms up, quiet, and stable. Don't look at your feet; look ahead. If you lean into the new direction too much, you will go shooting off to the side. Rebound in the other direction. This is a plyometric exercise, so you don't want to think about jumping over the bench as much as you want to think of immediately springing off of your toes.

Position two long benches parallel about three feet apart but displace the ends. Jump back and forth over the first, moving forward with each jump until you can land between them, then jump the second bench before going back again in a continuous movement. When you've really got rhythm, try jumping over both benches at the same time. Still too easy? Try throwing in a full turn with each single jump, but keep the same movement pattern.

LEAPFROG. This was fun then and it still is. You'll need some partners. Form a line with everyone facing straight ahead but in a good downhill tuck. The last person in line leapfrogs until he gets to the front, where he takes another step or two forward and sinks quickly into a tuck. The leapfrogger can push on the person in a tuck to try to unbalance him. The tucker can press up a little each time to try to spring the leapfrogger even higher. If done outdoors, the leapfrog

Ski fitness is for all ages. These juniors at a summer camp in Kaprun, Austria, develop lateral agility by jumping back and forth over a board.

Ski-intensive exercises can also be fun. This group of leapfroggers wandered up and down a few hills . . .

. . . before pairing off to run more hills piggyback style.

chain can ramble over some challenging terrain. Leapfrog is particularly hard when done uphill and potentially dangerous when going downhill.

TUMBLE JUMPING. Mats are preferable indoors, but outside, soft grass will work—better yet if it's a little muddy. Stand up, bend your knees, sit back, and roll gently onto your shoulders. Don't do a complete back tumbling roll, but stop with your legs curled up into your chest, crossed and directly overhead. Now roll forward quickly, place your front foot flat on the floor, and extend to stand up and finish with a jump. Don't use your hands to get upright. When you jump, cross your legs the opposite way, then sink back again onto the mat. You are now set up to extend off of the other opposite leg on the next forward roll.

ROPE JUMPING. This improves coordination and provides plyometric leg exercise. Some people don't

Every skier should have a good jump rope. There are many different jump-rope routines that will soon have you breathing hard.

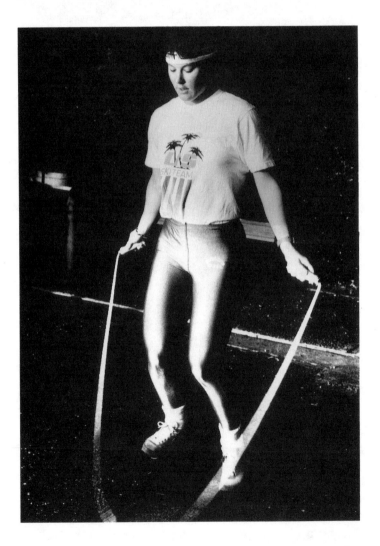

like to jump rope because they can't do it well. That isn't much of a reason. The most important thing is to get a good rope that isn't too light. I prefer one with short plastic sleeves along the length for weight. When you stand on the rope, the handles should come just under your armpits. Here are some variations:

Standard jump. Jump with feet together. Or, jump two repeats with the right leg and two with the left.

Bicycle jump. Alternate feet as fast as you can. Try to bring your knees to your chest.

Front and back jump. Jump with both feet together forward and back.

Side to side. Jump with feet together side to side.

Single-leg jumps. Skip rope on one foot.

Double jump. Twirl the rope twice around for each jump. Try to keep up a rhythm.

Crossovers. Just before you jump, cross your hands in front of you so the rope flips from one side to the other. This is easy if you keep your hands low.

CARIOCAS. These are another exercise staple of skiers. They help coordination and quickness and stretch the trunk. Run sideways, alternately crossing your legs as you cross the field. The goal is to keep your shoulders and chest facing ninety degrees to your direction of travel and to bring the hip around. For example, if you are running from left to right, as you swing your left leg across the right, rotate the left

To get the greatest benefits from cariocas, as you run sideways, move your hip as if it were a headlight shining perpendicular to your direction of travel.

hip around strongly as well so it faces the same direction as your upper body. Extend to the right with your right leg, then swing your left behind you and rotate the right hip out in front. Try running several repeats between ten- or twenty-yard-line markers.

BACKWARD RUNNING. It's not easy to run backward without occasionally tripping, particularly if you try it the ski-conditioning way. Ensure you have a

Running backward is a great way to condition legs and is useful to athletes recovering from knee injuries. Jeff Olson of the U.S. Ski Team keeps his hips low and slides his heels.

smooth field or an unobstructed court. When you run backward, keep a low position so that your knees are flexed and your hips are well behind your shoulders. Keep your head up and swing your arms in a straight line. Don't lift your feet as much as slide them by keeping your heels down. This provides extra resistance for the hamstrings and will help strengthen the knee. When you're out running some hills, take a few backward. This exercises the quadriceps.

DRUM MAJORS. You can run this exercise between twenty-yard-line markers or more. Tilt your torso slightly backward and extend one leg as high as possible. Try to get your toes above your head, but also stride as far forward as possible and stay up on your toes. If you land flat-footed, it will be difficult to get back off the ground quickly. The high-knee exercise is similar, but instead of extending the leg, bring the knee up as high as possible. In both exercises, speed is not as important as raising the leg or knee.

MOUNTAIN CLIMBERS. Assume a push-up position but with one leg extended and the knee of the other leg pulled up underneath to your chest. On "go," quickly alternate legs as if you were climbing a ladder. This works the hip flexors and hamstrings while isometrically working the shoulders.

BEND AND THRUST. This is known in most physical education courses as the infamous Burpee. Stand, flex in the knees, and drop straight until your hands touch the ground. Kick your legs out behind so that you are in a push-up position. Now pull your legs back in underneath and stand up with a strong jump. The Burpee wasn't much fun in high school and still isn't, but it's an excellent exercise for your shoulders, lower back, hip flexors, and quadriceps. Try pulling your legs up enough to shoot them through your arms, which will leave you in a sit-up position. Roll over onto your stomach and repeat.

TUCKING AND JUMPING. Skiers want to do most of their training dynamically, but skiing does involve times when the quadriceps are static.

When you are in a tuck, your back should be flat. Keep both feet straight ahead about shoulder width apart. Place your hands in front of your mouth with your elbows just touching, not resting, on your knees (form is important). For a very low tuck, spread your legs apart, try to keep your feet flat, and settle your torso down between your thighs. You can do this on very smooth slopes. Once in a tuck, do more than just grit your teeth. You can alternate through high, medium, and low positions; stand on one leg or the other; hop on both feet forward and back; hop on both feet side to side; and jump up out of a tuck and land back in one.

In conditioning for skiing, you should learn to jump off both feet and to land on both. The tuck and bench jumps help teach two-footed jumping. Most people

Hopping, skipping, jumping, bounding, and lunging activities are crucial to developing powerful legs for skiing. Members of the U.S. Ski Team take turns leaping to touch a goalpost crossbar.

have a dominant foot and prefer to jump off of that one. To become more balanced, run back and forth under a basketball hoop or football goalpost, and on each pass, take a big leap and try to touch the backboard, hoop, or crossbar. Try jumping off of one foot going one way and the opposite foot on the next pass. This is not as easy as it sounds.

COMBINED DRILLS. These achieve maximum intensity—continuous exercises that involve many of the single exercises listed above. If you have a watch with a countdown timer, set it for three to five minutes. Your basic position is the medium-low tuck. On "go," assume a tuck. The leader will call out different exercises to do every fifteen to thirty seconds. For example, do high/low tucks for forty-five seconds, then lunge walk for thirty seconds, tuck jump fifteen times, do mini-Girardellis for thirty seconds, tuck hop forward for thirty seconds, mountain climb for forty-five seconds, run backward for sixty seconds, and do more tuck jumps for thirty seconds. This would be an intense five-minute routine that would exercise many body segments. You can pyramid combined drills with consecutive three-, four-, and five-minute sessions, separated by breaks that allow the pulse to slow down to 100 to 120. After three or four such drills, you should be ready for a light stretch and a shower.

CIRCUIT TRAINING. This is similar to combined drills but requires more room. You establish a series of stations where you perform a certain amount of a specific exercise. These are fun in an open field where you run some distance between stations. Exercises might include push-ups, pull-ups, sit-ups, bend-and-thrusts, 100-yard dashes, and so forth.

RELAY RACES. Relay races can make hard workouts fun. Two teams of four people apiece are ideal. Any exercise makes a good stage in a relay race.

It's challenging to pose several tasks for each leg. For instance, the lead person for each team lies on his back. At "go," he must get to his feet without using his hands and run to midcourt. He then must put a hand down on the ground and twirl 360 degrees, then hop with both feet in a tuck to the far end, where he lies down, gets up without using hands again, and runs backward in a crouch to tag the next runner.

Balance and Coordination

All the exercises require balance and coordination, more so as you get tired. The next exercises concentrate on those skills.

FOOT HOOP JUMP. Try this one as you're stretching out. Stand and hold your right foot in your right hand (the quadricep stretch position). Try rotating your foot to the front without letting go of your toes or holding anything for balance. If you can do this, you're already better than average. Now notice that your right leg and arm form a hoop. Bend at the waist and try to jump your left leg through the hoop. Then try to jump back through. Rotate your leg, which is still being held by the toes, back to the starting position. You will usually find one side is much easier to do than the other.

BALL DRILLS. If you have access to a basketball court, dribbling develops eye-hand coordination. Make circuits of the court dribbling with one hand, then the other; switch hands after every bounce; dribble while running backward, left- and right-handed; dribble sideways; dribble with two balls at the same time, forward and backward; or dribble with two different balls, like a basketball and a volleyball. Try timed slaloms around people or cones. With a group, you can play dodgeball and keep-away. You can set up a slalom course and have everyone foot-dribble a soccer ball through it.

KIP. The kip can be done on the floor or on a high bar. On the floor, use a mat and, if possible, a spotter. Make sure you're well-stretched first. Lie on your back and pull your legs well back over your head. Place your hands palms down on the mat by your ears. As hard as you can, whip your legs forward while arching your back and pushing off with your hands. With enough spring, you should be able to land on your feet. The spotter can place a hand under your lower back and help lift so you get a little clearance underneath.

On a bar, pull yourself up chest high, then whip your legs up and over so that you rotate around the bar on your stomach. Concentrate on pulling your knees up as you arch back, leading with your shoulders and head. You can get some momentum by jumping up to the bar and continuing to pull through into the kip.

Like any other skill, balance can be improved. These athletes try to regain their balance after lunging onto one leg.

BALANCING. Balancing drills are challenging and can be frustrating. A simple one is done from the basic tuck position. Go to a high tuck and extend one leg into the air behind you. You will quickly feel your balance point. When you do, close your eyes. Bring your raised leg slowly out to the front. Go down to a low tuck, then back to a high. Change legs.

At some point, you can see what a little movement will do to enhance your balance. With eyes closed and balancing on one leg, bounce off of your toes a little. You should notice much better control with some moving about. The idea is that as long as you move smoothly, you can maintain better balance on your skis.

BONGO BOARD. Make your own board for next to nothing. All you need are a three-by-one-foot piece of half-inch plywood and a six-inch-wide piece of plastic pipe. Place the board on the pipe and balance on the board. This is best done outdoors. You'll quickly feel confident on this apparatus. Then you can add ball juggling!

TIGHTROPE. A backyard tightrope is easy to construct and will be a sensation for your party guests. The easy way is to tie a rope between two trees. Want something fancier? Set up two notched four-by-four posts, tie the ends of the rope to them, and secure the posts with a couple of guy wires and stakes. Get the

*Carolyn Curl improves her
balance by working out on a
bongo board.*

rope taut with a Z-pull arrangement using a climber's
pulley or with a trucker's hitch in the rope. Make sure
the rope is high enough that it doesn't touch the
ground when you stand on it. A bamboo slalom pole
helps when you're just learning to balance, but with a
little practice, you'll feel ready to run off with the
circus.

TALUS RUNNING. One of the psyching events of
early fall is a trip to the mountains. Before the rains
come, riverbeds usually are dry and some are great to

Dryland slalom incorporates tactics into an exercise session. As when skiing, keep your hands up and your upper body extended toward the outside of each turn. If you get sloppy, you'll soon lose traction and fall.

run along. Bases of cliffs or glacier edges are also excellent places to find large, smooth boulder fields.

Obviously, it's easy to twist an ankle, fall, or dislodge a rock on which you just jumped, but rock dodging and boulder hopping are fantastic for dexterity, agility, surefootedness, and learning to look ahead, focus, and concentrate.

DRYLAND SLALOM. With some bamboo poles, you can set up an easy slalom course. It's a good quickness and agility drill and always gets people fired up for skiing. Find a grassy hill that's not too steep. Putting rapid gates in grass makes rather large holes. You might consider resetting often so as not to totally destroy the grass.

Keep the weight on the downhill foot as you run around a gate. Try hopping only on the downhill foot as you round the pole, then make a sharp jump off that foot onto the uphill foot, run a few more steps, then hop again on the downhill foot.

SIX

Skiing Strength

STRENGTH TRAINING dates at least to ancient Greece. The wrestler Milo of Crotona, who lived in the early 500s B.C., was supposed to have lifted a young bull every day, and as the bull grew, so did Milo's strength, resulting in his winning the Olympic laurel crown six times.

There are few sports in which strength or weight training has not become essential. No other physical training has as much direct influence on improving skiing performance or enjoyment.

Strength training improves the speed and force of muscular contraction. Skiing at high speeds, you have to balance and counter greater forces. Shorter, sharper turns demand faster edge changes and fuller movements. Most elite competitors undergo rigorous weight training. The serious recreational skier also should incorporate these routines into preseason preparation.

Skiers may fear becoming muscle-bound, losing flexibility and speed. Today, there is no question that strength training improves agility and increases stamina, energy, vigor, and flexibility.

Women should participate, especially to develop more upper-body strength. On average, women's leg strength is 70% to 85% of men's, but they have only 40% to 60% of men's upper-body strength.

Find a good gym with a wide selection of weights and equipment, and a trainer who can develop a program for you and demonstrate proper technique. This doesn't have to be expensive; all you really need are a few machines, mirrors, and a good selection of free weights. It also helps to have a partner along as a spotter as well as to motivate you. It is difficult to work to your limits without a spotter.

What results should you expect when starting a strength-training program? Tim LaVallee, former ski coach of the University of Colorado, wrote in an article on strength training that 3% to 5% improvement per week was possible and a 50% improvement could be achieved in four to six months. Afterward, gains tend to be much slower. He also noted that strength endurance improves much faster than absolute strength.

Weight Training Basics

Sometimes, the gratification from weight training becomes the prime motivator. For lots of athletes, skiers included, the goal of gaining strength and power can change to the notion of just "getting big." There's nothing wrong with this, but if your goal is better skiing, take an occasional reality check to ensure that you are working toward that.

Remember, strength comes from progressive overloading of muscle groups. By definition, that means going beyond your present conditioning. It means tough, hard, heavy work that puts a deep burn in the muscle and leaves you limp and wrung out. Approach each workout with a positive, motivated attitude. When you're done, it's a great feeling.

It's inevitable that you will have good days when you feel as strong as a bull, and there will be times when you will have to drag yourself around the gym. Don't worry about the bad days. Try to work through as much of your program as possible, then get some rest. You will feel better as you work out, and overcoming adversity helps develop the athletic habit.

Approach each workout with a plan. Consider how much you want to do, the intensity, and how you feel. Anticipate how long it will take you to complete the exercises and try to stick to a schedule. It's easy to spend hours drifting from one station to another, socializing, and working out far less intensely than if you were methodical and quick. If someone is working at a station that is next in your routine, ask whether you can work in between that person's sets to keep your rhythm going.

THE PROGRAM. Begin each workout with some stretching and a fifteen- to twenty-minute aerobic workout on an exercycle, rowing machine, or stair climber. This raises your metabolism, which increases performance. A warmed-up muscle contracts more strongly, relaxes more completely, and is less prone to injury.

The order in which you do your exercises is important. Work large muscle groups first so that they get the appropriate overload. For example, do leg squats well before calf exercises. Also, work one body area completely before moving to another, and work opposing muscle groups. Muscles work as a system, not in isolation, so you must keep strength gains in balance.

Density refers to the amount of rest between sets of exercises. Keep a pace going without long rest periods. This will keep your muscles warm and your pulse and metabolism elevated. However, proper rest periods during a session are important to allow your muscles to refresh for another cycle.

Keep your program simple. You don't need more than ten to twelve exercises in any session, but you may want to switch exercises from one session to another or even split a routine, working the upper body one day and the lower body the next.

To avoid performance plateaus, "shock" the muscles from time to time so they don't get too comfortable with a given load or range of motion. You will probably have core exercises for large muscle groups, but it's important to exercise smaller ones, too. For instance, the leg press is crucial for skiers, but you may add side lunges with a loaded bar from time to time.

Do each exercise with strict form. If you concentrate on technique, a lighter weight will still get a serious pump into the muscle. You will force the muscle to contract at the beginning of the cycle, where the mechanical advantage is least, and work throughout a full range of motion, which builds flexibility and strength at all points throughout the contraction. As you tire during an exercise, you will recruit nearby muscles to assist in the movement.

At the end of a routine, you will probably throw in some body English to eke out the last few reps. That is not bad, but to keep the intended muscle group isolated, use a spotter on those "forced reps." This allows you to continue with good form and really work the muscle to its failure point.

LOADS, REPS, AND SETS. A lot has been written about the appropriate mix of load, repetitions, and sets to achieve maximum results. Consider the maximum weight you can lift in one repetition. Muscles work on an all-or-nothing basis. The fiber contracts fully or not at all, and at some point will become exhausted and need a brief rest. With somewhat less weight and more reps and sets, you will have to recruit many more fibers to compensate for those that become depleted. Research suggests that optimal gains are achieved with three to five sets of six to twelve reps.

There are many variations, such as circuit rotations and ladder progressions, but regardless of method, keep your program progressive, regular, and intense. Within about four weeks, you should notice increased vigor with better tolerance to exercise. Within eight weeks, you should definitely feel more strength and endurance. Adapt routines to accommodate what you feel you can do within the time you have to do it.

You may wish to try three or four sets of from eight to ten reps, using a spotter on the last two or three in the last set. Vary the weight among sets. If you can just bench press 200 pounds, the first set could be at 135, the second at 145, and the third at 155.

Proper breathing is important for maximizing each rep. The rule is to inhale on the rest stroke and exhale on the power stroke.

You hear a lot of grunting and bellowing as lifters finish a rep. Holding the breath and tensing the muscles throughout the torso gives the lifter momentary leverage. It also increases pressure in the chest and reduces the amount of blood returning to the heart, possibly causing dizziness or blackouts. Occasionally, lifters will have short but intense headaches, probably caused by a rapid increase in blood pressure. Many trainers recommend against this technique, but when working with heavier weights, it is virtually impossible not to hold your breath through the hardest part of the contraction. Try to exhale through pursed lips so you maintain some respiration.

Your spotter can help maximize each rep as you tire toward the end of an exercise. If you are doing arm curls and are close to muscle failure, your spotter could help you raise the barbell in the contraction phase, then continue to support it as you slowly lower it for another rep. This extra bit of support keeps your muscles contracted. This exercise is intense and should not be done with heavier weights than you would normally use.

The more you work out, the better you will know when to increase the load. You do so with more volume or intensity. Volume is the amount of work done through increased sets, reps, or number of exercises. This might be measured by calculating the amount of weight lifted in one session. For instance, with three sets times eight reps times twelve exercises, your total may be around fifteen tons. You can log this and compare from week to week.

Intensity relates to the work performed in a given time. If you do the same number of reps and sets but increase the speed or weight used, you've raised the intensity. Different training systems alter these variables and you need to evaluate them depending on your needs.

One simple method was devised by Alan Calvert in the early 1900s. An example for arm exercises would be to start with, say, five reps. At each training session, increase by one rep until you reach ten, then increase the load by five pounds and go back to five reps. (This straight-line approach may not work for someone who has been training for a while.) By reviewing your log, discussing your program with a trainer, and shocking the muscles into new adaptations, you will progress. The most important advice is to stick with it.

MAINTENANCE. At the first of the season, you may be in excellent shape, but if your only exercise is skiing, you may lose upper-body strength, and while leg strength may increase or stay the same, aerobic endurance may decline. To stay on top of your form, work out during the week, particularly if you only ski on weekends.

If you stop training, strength losses are modest over six to eight weeks, but some benefits can still be gained with a maintenance program of only one day a week. Initially, muscular endurance declines rapidly, but after three months, about 70% of endurance gained from training remains. Initial strength development requires a lot of work, but maintenance takes much less.

Muscle does not turn to fat when training stops. The structure of the tissues is permanently different. Muscles do one of two things, however: they get bigger and stronger or smaller and weaker, and fat more easily accumulates when exercising stops.

A diary keeps you focused on what you are doing, is a good indicator of your development, and can note periods when you are not recovering adequately. You should record your weight and dimensions periodically as well.

INJURIES. Done correctly, weight training is safe, especially compared with skiing. Most injuries occur from lack of warm-up, attempting heavy lifts without preparation, and occasional negligence. Besides muscle and tendon tears, tendinitis and bursitis are common and may require time away from the gym. The more you isolate a muscle and lock the joint, the more you risk injury.

Though you want to work out hard, you must protect yourself. If you feel sharp twinges at the joint or where the muscle attaches, stop. Move on, do similar exercises, examine your form, or use lighter weight. You may feel uncomfortable torque in your wrists when using a barbell. Use dumbbells or the bars with curved handgrips.

When attempting a new exercise for the first time, use a light weight and feel the range of movement. Get an idea of how much load you can lift. Certain exercises are riskier than others. For skiers, the popular leg extension machine puts a tremendous load on the knee joint at full extension. Consider one-leg knee bends holding onto a rubber cord on which you are standing, or hold a dumbbell in each hand, balance one foot on a bench behind you, and do partial one-legged knee bends.

A strong lower back is important for skiing, but when doing hyperextensions while lying prone, limit the exercise to the ninety degrees of motion from head down toward the floor to even with your legs. Dead lifts or good morning exercises should be performed with slightly bent knees to avoid hyperextension.

Free Weights and Weight Machines

Barbells and dumbbells are free weights because the lifter's movements are unconstrained. These and some cable-pulley devices were the tools of the trade until the mid-1970s, when Arthur Jones devised a machine to automatically vary resistance through a full range of muscle motion.

The machines have a cam resembling the shell of the nautilus, so that's what Jones named them. Because the cam provides varied resistance throughout its rotation, a muscle is taxed according to the force it can exert. Nautilus machines also stretch the muscle before each rep. This is intended to create a stronger contraction through the muscle's protective impulse to contract when stretched.

Other manufacturers have adopted the concept. Some Universal machines provide variable resistance with a fulcrum point that changes position through the exercise. The Cybex machine, used frequently in rehabilitation, provides resistance as long as you keep up with the rate of movement set by the user.

These machines are now a large part of any well-equipped gym, but there is continuing controversy over the merits of free weights versus variable-resistance devices. Both systems have advantages.

Muscles do have variable strength through a range of motion, but advocates of free weights note that they are challenged even in their strong positions by the natural acceleration of movement. Also, it takes coordination to lift free weights. They bring into play numerous muscle groups. You could load the plates up on a leg press machine, but it would be tough to lift the same weight in a squat because you need some of your strength to maintain your equilibrium.

This is important for skiers. They must exert force while balancing the entire system. Free weights allow you to exercise through a multitude of movements. Still, exercise machine routines can be learned quickly, and they cause fewer injuries because most have stops to keep them from bottoming out when you are exhausted. Again, machines are excellent for isolating specific muscles.

A good program will probably involve both free weights and machines. Switching back and forth can help you shock muscles. Lifters talk about avoiding performance plateaus by keeping the muscles "confused." Also, if you feel twinges in certain joints, you can often find a painless equivalent to an exercise by switching from machines to free weights or vice versa.

Most serious lifters use a belt. It supports the back and holds in the abdomen, against which you can exert tension and get more strength out of your lift. Belts should be considered particularly when doing squats.

Skiing Muscle Groups

Although skiing shares the physical needs found in other sports, it puts special demands on specific muscle groups. Most of the muscles essential to skiing attach to the pelvic girdle. Because all of these muscles must support one another, balanced strengthening of the midsection is extremely important. Regardless of how strong you are in one direction, you will be at a disadvantage if the opposing muscles are weak.

These terms are used in the descriptions:

Abduction: Movement away from the axis of the trunk, as in raising your leg to the side.

Adduction: Movement toward the axis of the trunk.

Flexion: Movement of two segments toward each other, pivoting at the joint.

Extension: Movement of two segments away from each other, pivoting at the joint.

HIP

Iliopsoas. When you pull your legs up to ski over a mogul, you use primarily the iliopsoas muscle, which flexes the femur on the pelvis, not the abdominals. When the femur is kept from flexing, the spine and pelvis flex on the femur and you do a sit-up.

Sartorius. This muscle is a long band that originates at the bottom of the pelvic crest and goes to the top of your tibia. As a two-joint muscle crossing both the hip and knee joint, the sartorius assists in flexion

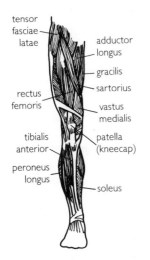

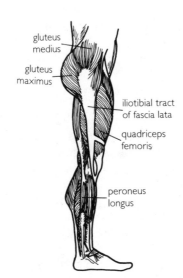

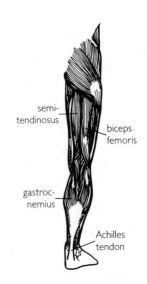

of the knee and hip. It is weaker when both actions are concurrent, as in skiing. By extending and anchoring both knees, it is exercised doing sit-ups.

Tensor fasciae latae. Another long muscle, it originates at the iliac crest and extends to the bottom of the thigh. For skiers, this is an important muscle, as it rotates the femur inward as it flexes, helping produce "knee angulation."

Rectus femoris. Among the quadriceps. See Knees.

Thigh adductors. There are six small muscles that connect the pelvis to the top of the femur. They pull the thigh toward the midline of the body and rotate the femur inward. For the skier, inward rotation of the femur in the hip socket plus knee flexion creates "knee angulation." These muscles are important for the performance skier, since heavy snow can throw a ski sideways, and a strong contraction of the inner thigh is needed to pull the ski back in. Explosive jumping and twisting off of one foot are good exercises.

Gluteus. The "glutes," muscles of your buttocks, are composed of the maximus, medius, and minimus. They attach at the top of the back of the pelvis and extend to the top of the back of the femur. The glutes are responsible for extending the thigh at the hip and lifting the leg out to the side. Running, hopping, jumping, and squats are all good glute exercises.

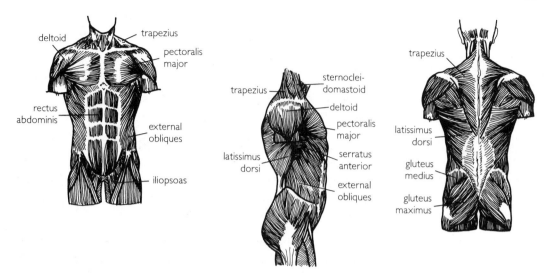

Hamstring. These are three muscles running down the back of the thigh. The semimembranosus, semitendinosus, and most prominent, the biceps femoris attach to the lower part of the pelvis and behind the knee on the tibia. They flex the lower leg and stabilize the knee. Strong hamstrings help prevent knee injuries; the three muscles wrap around to attach at the top of the shin.

KNEES

Quadriceps. When skiers think about getting in shape for the season, they give their quads a squeeze. These allow you to stand or jump out of a crouch. There are four major muscles in the group: the vastus lateralis, vastus medialis, vastus intermedius, and rectus femoris. The vastus muscles are attached to the kneecap and to the upper femur. The rectus femoris is attached just above the hip joint and to the lower end of the kneecap. The vastus muscles work alone to extend the lower leg when the hip is flexed forward. The rectus femoris comes into play when the hip is extended, as in skiing with your upper body erect.

THE TRUNK

Rectus abdominis. The abdominal muscles rival the quads as the most important muscles for skiers because they control the tilt of the pelvis and the arch of the back. Strong abs are the power link between the large muscles of the upper leg and the back. Skiers must have a good stance and solidly anchored pelvis for strong flexion and extension of the legs. The rectus abdominis are two long muscles that run from the fifth, sixth, and seventh ribs to the crest of the pubic bone.

Lateral obliques. These laterally flex and twist the trunk. Both sets help flex and rotate the trunk. The performance skier will want strong obliques for counterrotation or anticipation, and in extending himself over the downhill ski. These muscles along the side of the waist are formed by the external and internal oblique muscles. Working independently, they move the trunk from side to side.

Erector spinae. This is the muscle group of the lower back. For many skiers, even well-trained ones, these muscles are the most sore after the first few days of the season. They keep the upper body erect and so must have a lot of endurance. Skiers with weak lower backs chronically bend at the waist when the going gets tough.

The erector spinae extend along the spine. They are more efficient when the pelvis is held up in front, so again, strong abdominal muscles are important.

ANKLE AND FOOT

Tibialis anterior. Located on the front of the shin, this is often overlooked by skiers. It is the most prominent of several muscles in the front of the lower leg and raises the forefoot toward the tibia as well as raises the inside of the foot. When skiing powder or crud, or when you're caught back on the tails of your skis, these muscles are crucial for countering backward imbalance. Most skiers lever their bodies forward using their toes against the inside of their boots.

Gastrocnemius and soleus. These are among the calf muscles and raise the heel. They are developed by running, but since rigid boots do most stabilizing of the foot, calves don't get the same stress as muscles of the upper leg. Still, performance skiers who use a lot of subtle foot movement need good tone in the lower leg.

UPPER BODY. Many skiers wonder whether upper body strength is necessary for their sport. It is. The performance skier needs a well-muscled upper body to protect against injury in falls. Hiking out for un-tracked powder runs means strong chest, arms, and shoulders for poling and skating. Many preseason training programs require strength in the upper body. These groups won't be detailed, but exercises for the trapezius, deltoid, pectoralis, latissimus, biceps, tri-ceps, and muscles of the neck will be suggested in the next section.

Pumping Iron

Though there are exhaust*ing* exercises, an exhaust*ive* exercise program is practically impossible. The more you train, the more variations you will discover. Here are some of the key strength-training exercises you can do for skiing. Don't try to do all of them at any one session, and change them around for variety.

ABDOMINALS AND HIP FLEXOR ROUTINES. Your abs are used to a high volume of work at low intensity. Enough weight to fatigue them after only eight to ten reps would likely put too much stress on the back, so it is best to train with more reps.

Contraction of your abdominal muscles shortens the distance between the sternum and pelvis, and has no direct role in raising your knees up to the chest as in a straight-leg sit-up. When doing any of these exer-cises, pay attention to how your back feels and adjust your routine accordingly. Be sure to exhale during peak contraction. The rectus abdominis muscles help the diaphragm contract. If you inhale, your lungs will act as a cushion and prevent maximum contraction of the abdominal muscles.

Machines. The Nautilus abdominal machine is ex-cellent. It isolates the rectus abdominis by securing your feet under the seat. You bend forward at the waist by pulling the ring attached to the articulated seat back forward and down. Resistance is adjusted with plates. You can get somewhat the same exercise with rope crunches. Attach a short rope to the vertical cable pull on a Universal machine. Hold the rope behind your head, sit upright on your knees, and bend for-ward through the abdominals.

Calisthenics. Most abdominal exercises are per-formed using only body weight, though you can in-crease resistance using incline or decline boards, or by placing a small weight behind your neck. Because

Strong abdominal muscles and hip flexors are essential for performance skiing. Exercises like crunches can be tailored to work specific abdominal muscle groups.

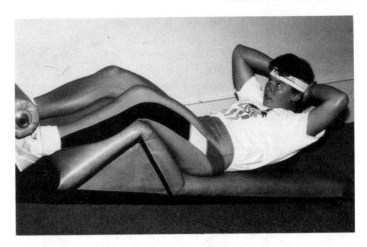

many of these exercises are done without weights, try to increase your speed, which increases the amount of force required. You can count reps or do each exercise for, say, thirty to sixty seconds to make up one set.

Crunches. Lie on your back with your knees pulled up. Interlace your hands behind your head. Raise your shoulders off the ground to touch knees with elbows.

Heel-high sit-up. Lie on your back with your knees bent and your lower legs on top of a bench. Lace your hands behind your head and raise your shoulders off the floor as high as you can. If the bench also has a foot restraint, you can lift your upper body off the floor by flexing at the waist.

Bicycles. Lie on your back and lace your hands behind your head. Alternately pull each knee up to your chest and touch it with the opposite-side elbow.

Seated leg raises. Sit on the edge of a bench and lean back, holding the sides of the bench behind you for balance. Extend your legs and raise them as high as you can.

Hanging crunches. Hang upside down with your knees over a padded bar. Have a spotter hold your lower legs, and curl as high as you can.

Cherry pickers. Lying on your back, raise your legs straight up. Alternately reach with one hand to the opposite toe, lie back, then touch your other toe with the other hand.

Lying leg raises. Lie on your back and do a variety of

timed raises, such as legs together; legs apart; feet six inches high, then twelve inches high; flutter kick; and leg crossover. To preserve your lower back, place your hands under your buttocks.

Resistance leg raises. Lie on your back and have a partner hold your ankle. Raise and lower one leg for a set period. Switch legs. This can stress the back, so place your hands under your buttocks.

Nate Bryan of the U.S. Ski Team holds the feet of a teammate performing sit-ups on a gymnastics bar. This is an advanced abdominal exercise.

Leg lifts done in a Roman chair target and develop the hip flexors.

Bar leg raises. Hang from a bar and do straight-leg raises. To work your abs, concentrate on pulling your pelvis forward and up. This primarily exercises the hip flexors, but you will engage the abs if you concentrate on rounding your back. You probably will be able to do just a few of these, so get a spotter to help raise your legs and also to resist on the downswing. This is very intense.

Emilys. Lie on your back with your legs straight up. Extend your arms to the side for balance. Alternately lower your legs from one side to the other.

Jouberts. Balance on your buttocks with your legs together extended in front of you and both arms extended out and to one side. As you pull your knees into your chest, bend your arms and pass your hands around to the other side, bringing them over your navel. Once your hands have crossed over, extend both your legs and arms once more, all the time remaining balanced on your buttocks.

Crossover sit-ups. Lie on your left side and cross your right leg over the left with the right knee up. Sit up to touch your right elbow to your right knee. After a set, switch sides.

Partner side sit-ups. Lie on your side and have a partner hold your feet and calves down. With hands behind your head, raise up sideways as far as you can. You can also do this on a back extension bench by lying sideways and hooking your feet under the restraint.

Side bends. Stand up with your feet shoulder-width apart. Hold a dumbbell in one hand as you flex from one side to the other.

Overhead toe touches. Lie on your back and raise your legs straight back over your head and touch your toes to the floor behind your head. Don't do this without substantial warm-up or if you have any back problem.

QUADRICEPS AND GLUTEUS. Except for lower leg extensions, the gluteus muscles are brought into play every time you do quadricep exercises with more than a fifteen-degree flexion of the leg at the hip.

Leg press. The leg press machine is excellent for getting started, since you can load a lot of weight to develop leg strength, but there's no risk or need for a spotter as when doing squats. This exercise is easier at the top, so don't throw the rack up off your feet and lock your knees out; keep the knees slightly bent and the weight always floating. Warm into this one on at least the first set by only bringing the weight down a short distance, then gradually increasing the range of motion.

By changing the position of your feet, you can emphasize different leg muscles. For instance, pointing your toes works the adductors. Presses with the feet inward work the tensor fasciae latae, important for knee angulation. Use lighter weight when your legs are not in a strong, straight line.

Kelly McCann, former professional racer and 1990 NASTAR National Champion, begins his leg routine with the leg press machine. By inclining the backboard nearly ninety degrees, he further isolates his leg muscles.

With good knees, performance skiers should be able to press about twice their body weight at least once. Dr. George Twardokens says top racers can press nearly three times their body weight.

Squats. The squat is the king of exercises for skiers because it works the thighs, hips, and glutes simultaneously. You also must use good technique. Because so much weight can be used, some fear knee and back problems, but with good form and practice, this exercise is safe. Use a wood bar to practice in a mirror, then use light weights until you feel the right range of movement. Center a padded bar on the trapezius muscles (the lower part of your shoulders). Keep your heels flat, with toes pointed slightly outward five to ten degrees and knees projecting out over your feet. Keep your back erect without rounding it by looking at a point on the wall above your head. Never bounce at the bottom of the squat. Your shoes should have good lateral support so your feet won't roll off them. If you have trouble keeping your balance, consider elevating your heels with a two-by-four under your heels. Consider wearing a weight belt to help support the lower back and abdomen. Some lifters like to wrap the knees, too.

With a little lighter weight, you can perform squats with the weight across your chest instead of your back. This variation requires more balance. Hold the bar with either conventional or crossbar grip. By going

When doing squats, keep your knees directly over your feet and your head up. Be careful when performing this exercise; McCann wears a belt whenever squatting more than his body weight.

deep on the squat, you will exercise the gluteus muscles.

Leg extensions. These popular exercises isolate the quadriceps very well. Some trainers discourage this device, however, because seated on the machine, your knee is solidly anchored and the vastus of the quadriceps do most of the work, which applies a lot of stress on the knee joint. This exercise should be done slowly or at a lighter weight with more reps. Don't throw the weight at the top of your extension. If you experience

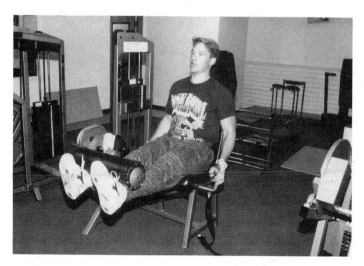

The leg extension is a good machine for developing leg strength, but can cause knee pain if overdone. Vary your leg routine so that you can skip this exercise from time to time.

One-legged knee bends with dumbbells can effectively work your quadriceps without heavy weights. Be careful not to bend your leg more than ninety degrees.

knee pain, discontinue this exercise. For an alternative, stand on one foot with your other foot resting on a bench behind you for balance. Hold a couple of dumbbells and do one-legged quarter or half knee bends.

Drive-ups. Place a barbell with a padded collar low on your shoulders. Step up onto a bench high enough so your thigh is ninety degrees to the floor. Alternate each leg.

The lunge. Place a barbell with a padded collar low on your shoulders. Now step forward with one foot,

Drive-ups are a variation of the squat and the lunge. Perform this exercise smoothly, always using a light weight and maintaining control.

Lunges develop leg strength and control. Use a light weight, keep your back straight, and drop onto your rear knee slowly to avoid banging it against the floor.

allowing your other knee to sink toward the floor. Tilt the head and chest back and drive up, alternating legs. The lunge isolates the quadriceps, glutes, and groin muscles. Though similar to squats in effect, you need power and balance for this exercise.

Side lunges. You don't see this much at gyms unless skiers are around. The weight is centered over each leg to isolate the quadricep. Do this slowly to avoid stressing the groin.

Adductor-abductor press. You'll need a machine. Seated, spread your legs and position the pads inside your thighs near your knees. The deep-thigh adductors will benefit from bringing the pads together. (Don't use a lot of weight on this one, at least for starters, as these muscles don't normally get a lot of exercise.) Sitting on the edge of the seat, you can exercise the abductors one at a time by positioning the pad on the outside of the knee and pressing it away from you.

Rear leg raises. Put a collar around your ankle and connect it to a cable machine that has a pulley close to the floor. Hold onto a bar (there's usually one on the machine) and back up a bit to tense the cable so you can bend slightly at the waist. Facing the cable, raise your leg straight behind you. You can usually load about as much weight for one leg as you can for both legs doing leg curls. This is good for the gluteus and the sacrospinalis. If you haven't done it before, you will probably feel it the next day.

Tibialis dorsi flexion. This exercise works the tibialis anterior muscle. Sit on the floor. Attach a collar around the foot and clip it to a horizontal cable pull. Flex the foot at the ankle toward the shin. You can also get a good workout with a partner providing resistance by holding your foot.

Partner tucks. Assume a tuck and have a partner of about your own size climb onto your back with his weight resting over your lower back and hips. From this position, you can move up and down from a low to a high tuck. A few minutes of this will put a good burn into your thighs.

HAMSTRINGS

Lying leg curl. Lie flat on the machine's bench with the roller resting on the Achilles tendon. Keep the hips flat, though with heavy weight, some pelvic tilt will be inevitable.

Standing leg curls. The standing curl machine reduces the stress on your back. When you bend the knee, there will be hip flexion, but standing, your hips can move more freely and not transmit the force to the

Leg curls can stress your lower back, so use an articulated bench whenever possible. Strong hamstrings will balance the power of your quadriceps.

lower back. This machine gives you peak contraction when the lower leg is at ninety degrees to your body, because the roller is in line with gravity.

LOWER BACK

Seated rows. Before doing this exercise, get the feel for the movement on a rowing machine. You can load a fair amount of weight on, so you want good form. Sit holding onto the cable handles. Reach forward without much rounding of your back and keep your knees slightly bent. Lean back slightly with your upper body and pull your arms in to hold the handles at your abdomen at the end of the exercise. This will also exercise your lat, serratus, and trapezius muscles.

Standing dead lifts. Stand on a box or bench when doing this exercise so you have more range of motion. This exercise strongly stretches the lower back and hamstrings. You may wish to keep the knees slightly bent to reduce pull on these muscles. Slow movement and strict form are important. By not standing erect at the top of the movement, you can keep the load on the muscles, use lighter weight, and avoid stress to the lower back.

Back raise. Lie facedown on a bench so that your

Dead lifts should be done with light weights and high repetitions until you are comfortable with the movement. McCann uses a reverse grip to improve his balance.

The back raise is a good exercise for strengthening lower back muscles and avoiding the pain experienced by many skiers. Carolyn Curl holds a ten-pound weight across her shoulders to increase the intensity of her workout.

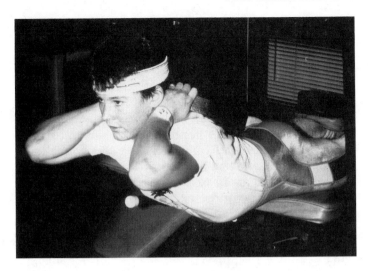

pelvis is on the table and your legs are held down. Let the trunk bend forward and then extend your spine just until your trunk is in line with your body. Going farther would hyperextend your back, stressing the vertebrae. Start without weight and one or two sets of twenty. As it becomes easier, try holding some weight behind your neck. Keep the movements slow and controlled.

UPPER BODY. It's not enough to work on your lower body. You need muscular balance throughout. Also, you derive strength not just from shocking muscles in isolation, but by putting demands on your entire constitution, enervating your nervous system, speeding up your metabolism, and building mass. Here is a short list of some good upper-body exercises. You will want to expand your repertoire as you go along.

Bench press. This is a good free-weight exercise. Have a spotter help on maximal loads. Keep your hands slightly wider than your shoulders and concentrate on keeping your back flat on the bench.

Lat pull. Bring the bar behind your head, concentrating on the latissimus muscles. Pull through your elbows, keeping them in line with your torso. When you're tired, pull the last few reps down to your chest instead of behind your neck.

Military press. By using dumbbells, your arms can rotate through their natural range—your palms will

Upper-body strength will help prevent injury in hard falls. The bench press is a basic exercise that can be varied by using different grips and decline or incline boards.

face your ears at the bottom of the movement, then face outward at the top.

Pec deck flyes. For better isolation of the pectoralis muscles, use a machine for this exercise. Go light at first, as the machine will stretch your pecs a lot at the attachment points. Lying on the bench with free weights, you use your arms a lot and overstretch the muscles when your arms are extended in the weak position at the sides.

Keep your back straight when performing lat pulls. As with all exercises, the quality of each repetition is as important as the amount of weight used.

When doing curls with a curl bar, you can use grips of different widths to work the various aspects of the biceps muscle.

Arm raises. To strengthen the deltoids, use light weight, then raise your arms straight up from the sides over your head. Repeat by raising your arms straight in front of you.

Curls. These exercises can be performed many ways. You can isolate the arms doing preacher curls, use dumbbells, barbells with straight or bent grip, or use a curl machine. Try different methods and progressions to see what works best for you. Watch for

To isolate the proper muscles when performing triceps pressdowns, hold your elbows against your body and control the bar at all times.

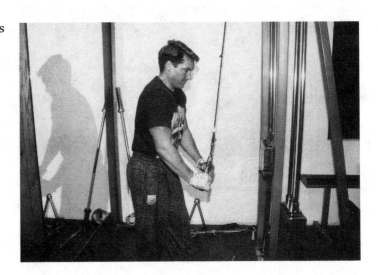

stress in the wrist tendons when doing lots of curls, particularly when isolating the arm with benches.

Triceps pressdown. Whenever you have to pole across long flats or uphills, you will remember this exercise thankfully. Curl your wrists over the top of the pressdown bar so they are not in a weak position. Push down with elbows in tight. After the press, control the bar coming up and stop it when it reaches chest height. After pressdowns, try some dips with a spotter to raise your legs. Vary the exercise on occasion by attaching a rope instead of the bar.

Pumping Rubber

Building the quadriceps specifically for skiing can be difficult. The popular leg extension stresses the knee. To conserve the knees while still getting a good quad workout, use a Sport Cord or surgical tubing. Stand on the cord, flexing at the knee. Hold one end at midthigh with one hand and hold a chair back for balance in the other. Perform slow one-third knee bends. The cord creates constant resistance going up as well as down. Place the cord around your waist and secure the other end in a door jamb. When you jump to the side, you create tension. This movement forces you to land with the leg closest to the door in a braced position, just like edging the downhill ski.

Protecting Knees

You can't really improve the strength of ligaments; it's hereditary. But muscles around the knee can be strengthened. Three important long muscles (sartorius, gracilis, and semitendinosus) that all start in the pelvis come together on the inside of the upper shin. They, along with the hamstring, help protect the medial collateral ligament, which is frequently damaged in knee injuries. If you do too much too soon, you will feel it in your joints. To prepare cartilage and tendons, many professional bodybuilders use lighter weight and more reps for a time before periods of heavy lifting.

SEVEN

When the Snow's Gone

EVEN THE BEST ski seasons are only about six months long, unless you camp on Mount Hood in the summer. But for serious skiers, skiing never really ends; it just changes shape. Skiing is something much more fundamental than two slats on snow. It's the sublime feeling of being in motion, in control. It's being the center of energy in a dance. You become a juggler of nature's forces: velocity, mass, gravity, centrifugal force, friction. It's an art form in a most Zen sense, because you use these forces like paints to create a pattern and image, but take nothing material from the creation, only thoughts and feelings.

So when the snow is gone, skiers don't just look for something to take the place of skiing; they look to re-create the primal flowing sensation. Though nothing may beat skiing, there are a number of activities that ring the same chimes. Every sport makes its own demands of you, but any skier recognizes the mental and physical associations you can make between skiing and other outdoor sports.

Following are several sports that, in their own way, can help maintain that skiing rush. Familiarity breeds competence. Also, remember that anything you do in the off-season should be fun. Don't do it for the sake of

After a day of summer skiing on Mount Hood, these young athletes play an impromptu game of volleyball, another great sport for sharpening reflexes and developing leg power.

your skiing mentality. Off-season sports keep the competitive spirit alive and may help you unravel the techniques of something completely new.

Each of these sports can take a lifetime to master, but the following comments should introduce you to the basic nature of each sport.

Bounding on a trampoline is a fun way to enhance kinesthetic awareness and body control. For more advanced flips and twists, the athlete can be spotted with a harness strung from the overhead rig.

In-line Skating

Skiers have always looked for some summer sport that emulates the skiing experience. Grass skis, skiing simulators, and indoor minimountains have been tried, but in the last few years, in-line skates have become popular.

In-line skates typically have four (three on the smaller sizes or cheaper models, five on racing models) high-density rubber wheels turning on precision bearings. As long as you're upright, it's a non-impact exercise, so skating is easier on the knees than running. Skating is a great way to maintain coordination and build strong gluteus and quadricep muscles. Also, turning techniques on downhill sections are equivalent to those in skiing, though at slow speeds you can carve more precisely on skates than on skis.

The crossover step helps you accelerate and forms the basis for more advanced maneuvers. Always wear protective pads when skating.

Road riding is a great way to stay in shape, but pedaling is tightly constrained and efficiency comes from steady bike handling. Mountain biking pushes your aerobic and anaerobic systems to their limits and requires agility, balance, and concentration. Like a skier picking his line through a sea of moguls, the mountain biker on a steep descent has to make split-second decisions to keep a safe line.

Mountain Biking

Some people suggest basketball as an off-season sport for skiers. The Mahre twins were excellent players, for example. I prefer soccer as a team sport requiring stamina, agility, and coordination, primarily because at five-foot-seven, I've always gotten clobbered at basketball. Lacrosse and rugby also would be good off-season sports, along with ultimate Frisbee, team handball, hockey, tennis, squash, racquetball, and tournament badminton.

For the sake of argument, take basketball for a moment. As you're running down a cramped court, you have to figure your traveling speed, timing in dribbling, the speed of your oncoming opponent, potential escape routes, the speed of the teammate to whom you may pass, and the range to the basket. It's a lot of brain activity to conduct at full tilt.

In soccer, you have to coordinate the feet for dribbling, aiming, and passing while keeping your bal-

Soccer

Soccer develops coordination, speed, and endurance. Because it requires explosive bursts of speed, it does more for your skiing fitness than jogging can.

ance. It also is extremely strenuous. One study of the British Olympic soccer team showed players covering 12,000 to 16,500 yards during a match, 25% at speed, which calls for a strong anaerobic system. The distance is not inordinate, but the starting, stopping, jumping, turning, and getting off the ground put an extra load on the body. It is certainly easier to run straight than to stop and turn.

Water-skiing

In some ways, water-skiing has a lot more in common with surfing than snow skiing. There is little hip angulation in turns, just body inclination. There are similarities, too, though. Speeds of thirty to seventy miles per hour are equivalent to fast cruising or giant slalom skiing. Carving, unweighting, rotation, edge changing—the familiar terms of alpine skiing—are used by water-skiers. The skier must balance strong forces, so there is a premium on hip, quadricep, lower back, chest, shoulder, and arm strength. Competition slalom skiers may resist loads upward of 400 pounds in a strong pull across the wake. Great water-skiers are smooth and efficient, but they are essentially playing tug-of-war with the boat.

Water-skiing demands all the concentration and strength of alpine skiing, as Gregg Tate, a top competitive water-skier, demonstrates.

Martial Arts

All the martial arts develop coordination, timing, mental focus, and confidence, since they are the study of effective movement in the most demanding arena of all—hand-to-hand combat.

There are dozens of schools of martial arts and hundreds of forms. There is no answer to the question, "Which is best?" There are only levels of proficiency. You may wish to consider which school best reflects your personality.

There are soft and hard martial arts. There is no distinct line, as many schools take aspects of both, but hard style is typified by ballistic kicking and punching. Some well-known hard martial arts schools are the Korean tae kwon do, Okinawan karate, and jeet kun do, which Bruce Lee developed. Soft styles involve blending with and controlling the power and momentum of the opponent to your advantage. These demonstrate avoiding, throwing, pinning, choking, and immobilizing. T'ai chi and aikido are soft martial arts. Jujitsu falls in the middle, effectively combining striking and throwing.

Having trained in both styles, I would recommend

John Atkins, former U.S. Ski Team conditioning coach and holder of a black belt in karate, shows his athletes some basic techniques.

judo and aikido to skiers who want to concentrate on movement and balance.

Board Sailing

Some say that board sailing may become the official sport of the U.S. Ski Team. From the end of ski season to the start of the school year, thousands of skiers take up board sailing along the Columbia River Gorge in Oregon. You don't have to go all the way to the Gorge to sail; anyplace with strong wind and an open body of water will do. Sailing's best in spring and fall when the winds come up.

High-wind sailing on short boards is very different from light-air long-board sailing. Skiers balance against gravity and centrifugal force; board sailers must balance against the pull of the sail. There's plenty of speed in board sailing, along with high-flying jumps. Instead of using a stiff boot to stabilize the foot, the board sailer uses a harness and foot straps.

Board sailing has become a very popular off-season activity for skiers because it rewards good technique and stamina with plenty of excitement.

Maylon Hanold, member of the U.S. Whitewater Team, clears a slalom gate and exits an eddy by using proper technique.

Kayaking

Skiers sometimes give whitewater kayaking short shrift. Maybe they consider it oddball, like bungee jumping. This is unfortunate, since serious skiers are discovering the joys of this sport along with similarities between whitewater paddling and alpine skiing. Several members of the U.S. Ski Team have taken up the sport for relaxation.

Whitewater paddling is a gravity sport done in the mountains, and like skiing, it is complex and combines physical strength, stamina, technical skills, and tactical savvy. It is an excellent complement to skiing for the mountain athlete, as it exercises the upper body after a long skiing season of relative neglect. Also, the whitewater season commences at the time skiing is winding down. Like good skiers, good paddlers develop strong abdominal muscles, hip flexors, arms, shoulders, and backs.

EIGHT

Training Plans

FITNESS FOR SKIING requires conditioning, and unless you have a trust fund or are an elite racer, time for it is scarce. Recreational athletes exercise when they can and, come skiing season, they go with whatever they've achieved.

Maybe you can't find more time for conditioning this year, but you can make the time you do have more effective. You can attain higher performance with a logical progression for your workouts.

When coaches design training programs, they first look at time frames. At the most basic level, there is a plan for that day. Athletes also have weekly plans, so they know which days to train hard, which days are light, which are devoted to coordination and balance, and which are for rest. Unless you race or have experience with other organized sports, the weekly plan is about as far as most people go.

More comprehensive plans involve weekly training in cycles of a month or more, known as macrocycles, to cover the year. Cyclical training builds the athlete from the base up, starting with general sports and culminating in skills specific to a sport. On even larger scales, elite athletes formulate two- or four-year cycles

Ski-specific conditioning programs are not just for racers. This group of recreational skiers meets four times a week each fall for informal but intense training sessions.

to peak for Olympic or world championship competition. In the Eastern bloc, training plans of up to sixteen years were developed to bring children up to the top of international competition by their early twenties.

This is a discussion of a simple cyclical approach to conditioning for an upcoming ski season. If you begin planning in midsummer, you can make excellent gains by Thanksgiving. For the recreational skier, this may seem a little premature; most skiers don't really get going until October. There are three things to keep in mind:

1. Three or four months of preparation for many sports is to be expected. For instance, if you already have a good base, most experts recommend at least ninety days to prepare just to complete a marathon. Doesn't a months-long skiing season deserve just as much time? It may not even be as difficult as it sounds. The method suggested here breaks the year up into increments so that you can get a better understanding of where you are in the fitness spectrum.

2. By starting early and letting your body adapt gradually, you will be much more comfortable later during the intense conditioning phase.

3. Conditioning can be fun or it can be a chore. One

Targeting a specific heart-rate range will make your exercises more effective. Performance skiers should develop their aerobic endurance during the summer and work toward more intense anaerobic sessions as the ski season approaches.

Level	Zone	Method	Percent of maximum heart rate
I	Aerobic endurance	Easy–medium distances	60–85
2	Anaerobic threshold	Easy pace intervals	85–90
3	VO$_2$ Max	Hard pace intervals	90–95
4	Anaerobic	Hard intervals	95–100

way to keep it fun is by working out in a group. End each workout with the feeling that you can do a little more.

The better shape you're in, the more your energy will increase and the more you will look forward to exerting yourself. Enhanced fitness can undeniably elevate mood, increase confidence, and create energy.

The Annual Plan

A year's training should include at least five cycles: active rest, preparation, maximum strength, conversion, and maintenance. The competition skier would also have a competition cycle, and perhaps a precompetitive cycle.

Active rest extends from the end of the season to the beginning of the three conditioning cycles. The first, or preparation cycle, sets you up for more intense workouts by exercise-proofing your body. Skiing is a power sport: It involves strength and speed. You should develop as much strength as possible in the second conditioning period. In the conversion cycle, you apply your strength to power and endurance with high-intensity agility and stamina exercises. Finally, the maintenance cycle takes you through the season with exercises to keep you flexible and retain your gains of the preseason.

You can lengthen or shorten these periods to match the time you have and your skiing goals. Skiing is fun. When it stops being that, it's time to do something else.

Of course, you must make any plan fit your athletic profile, but you should still incorporate all five cycles into your year. To figure the lengths of these periods, take a late summer starting time and then divide the number of days between then and the start of the season (say, Thanksgiving) by three—the preparation, maximum strength, and conversion periods. This gives you about a month per period. You must buffer each cycle with a week to recuperate with active rest, so this leaves three weeks per period.

If you are already in good shape, your preparation period might be shortened by a week, which you could add to the maximum strength cycle. Competitors or fitness junkies might want four to six weeks per period. If you are beginning to exercise close to the season and have done little during the summer, exercise in the preparation cycle manner. Conversion cycle training without preparation will lead to injuries.

You can formalize these periods with logs and graphs, or you can casually acknowledge period changes with an X on the calendar. It has to suit your mentality, but never forget that you get out of it what you put into it.

In general, the amount of exercise increases rapidly in the preparation period but the intensity is low. In the maximum strength period, volume drops and intensity increases dramatically, but maximum strength cannot be developed without proper preparation. In the conversion cycle, less time is devoted to weight training and more to power exercises specific to skiing.

These periods are not mutually exclusive. Each simply emphasizes an aspect of your fitness. Involve all aspects of training in each period throughout the annual cycle. For example, incorporate some endurance training during the conversion cycle for variety.

ACTIVE REST CYCLE. For most skiers, the active rest period extends from mid-April through August. For racers, it may be a lot shorter, maybe one to two months immediately after the previous season. During this time, you keep busy with other sports, such as the ones mentioned in Chapter Seven, and enjoy running and weight training for their own sake.

There is no reason to keep skiing on your mind, and most skiers don't have a problem putting it behind them during the off-season. This is an important rite of spring. In doing so, come late August, you will start feeling the itch again. During the active rest cycle, the accent is on fitness through sport, not conditioning.

All aspects of fitness come into play: aerobic and an-aerobic exercise, flexibility, balance, coordination, agility, strength, and power.

PREPARATION CYCLE. This important phase prevents injuries later in your program. You assess your current condition, attend to any rehabilitation, and strengthen tendons and ligaments. As mentioned before, this period involves a lot of low-intensity exercise, but sessions will still be demanding.

Now is the time for your physical, particularly if you are over thirty-five. Test your fitness and log the results so that you can check your progress. Also, check for muscular imbalances. Everyone has a dominant arm or leg, and skiing requires bilateral dexterity. Any disparities should be noted. Check your posture. Strip down in front of a full-length mirror to see whether one shoulder or hip is higher than the other. Do your knees or feet point in the same direction? Postural imbalances can harm strength and coordination and cause chronic back, hip, or shoulder pain. If you suspect you have some postural discrepancies, consult a qualified physical therapist or rolfing expert.

Check for your dominant leg in a gym. Set the weight on a leg extension machine for about 70% of your one-repetition maximum (1 RM) for one leg. Compare the number of reps you can do with each leg, then move over to the leg curl machine and test your hamstrings. For your upper body, use dumbbells for curls and triceps extensions. To correct any imbalances, add a few reps to the weak side during your conditioning sessions.

Ligaments and tendons take longer to strengthen than muscles, so maybe your muscles can take the strain but the connective tissue can't. During the preparatory phase, exercise with light weights and lots of reps, as many as twenty or more in four to six sets. Good form during this phase isolates each muscle group as much as possible and sets the proper range of motion. Don't forget to warm up and stretch completely.

If you run, keep the distance short (three to five miles) so that you can push your pace. You might carry hand weights. Instead of cycling five or six hours on a weekend, ride at a more intense pace for one to one and a half hours. Do short intervals of near-maximum power when running or cycling.

Start emphasizing the abdominal and midsection muscles. The abs can withstand a lot of exercise if the intensity is low, and don't neglect the lower back.

At the end of this cycle, you should feel your body responding to the increased load. Take a week of active rest to recuperate and prepare yourself for the next cycle.

MAXIMUM STRENGTH CYCLE. This period emphasizes high-intensity weight lifting and anaerobic exercises. You must stretch daily and build agility. Training for each exercise would require five sets of six to twelve reps. Your muscles will respond with weight of at least 66% of 1RM. If you've gone through the preparation phase without incident, you shouldn't have too much trouble at 75% of 1RM. You should be able to figure what 1RM would be for each exercise by the number of reps you can do at less weight; however, if you do want to determine 1RM, use free weights and have spotters to help rack the weight.

Avoid the "gym rat syndrome." You have seen jocks who spend four hours or more every day in the gym. They usually have great muscles, but only exceptional bodybuilders need more than one to two hours of weight training a day. With sufficient weight, correct technique, and minimum dawdling, your body should tell you that enough is enough after ninety minutes. During this time, you can warm up, stretch, and do eight to ten training routines.

To apply maximum intensity, split routines. Spend one day on your upper body, the next on your lower. At this intensity, your body should also tell you that it does not want to work on the same muscles for another forty-eight hours.

In addition, several sessions each week should be done at a field or indoor gym. Track work, such as 220s and 440s done pyramid-fashion, will help enervate fast-twitch muscles and develop leg speed. Hill and stair running in bursts are good alternates to track work on different days. Speed hikes up ski trails and mountain bike rides on weekends are also excellent conditioners. Again, at the end of this phase, take a week to recuperate with active rest.

CONVERSION CYCLE. The conversion period is particularly challenging, physically and mentally. It takes your new strength and couples it with speed so that you can generate maximum force in minimum time. During this phase, you use high-intensity repetitions of sixty to ninety seconds. You re-create as many skiing motions as possible. In your weight-training routines, reduce the weight you've been using but increase the number of reps to twelve to fifteen and the sets from four to six. While increasing the weight each week, do each lift quickly, with good form and always with control.

Daylight is rapidly diminishing, so you will probably conduct most of your training indoors. Agility and coordination exercises should become more intense. Tuck jumps, bounding, hopping, leaping, and lunge walking and jumping, done for sixty to ninety seconds forward, backward, and laterally, will put a deep burn in the muscles. An exercise like Girardellis should be a regular drill at each session. A typical workout might involve a dozen of these exercises over thirty to forty yards.

Plyometric exercises come into play now. Bench jumping is a favorite; it is taxing and takes skill. Even if you are in good shape, be careful while doing plyometrics.

The intensity of power training makes you vulnerable to injury and illness, and at the least you will be stiff and sore. This is particularly annoying because you may feel that time off for recovery sets back many of the gains you have made so close to the season. Because power training is so taxing, take extra care to log your daily rest and active heart rates; weight; condition of joints, muscles, and tendons; and feelings of energy or fatigue. The art of conditioning comes from overloading your system, with just enough recovery. Too little recovery time, and your performance will drop and you may become injured.

MAINTENANCE CYCLE. By now, you're skiing and are amazing your friends and yourself with your energy and vitality. You may be skiing three or four days a week, but you still need to keep up your strength and endurance through regular weekly workouts. They need not be long or intense. If you ski hard, maintenance sessions can be light-day routines. They should include stretching and some high-rep strength workouts to avert muscle imbalances. Don't use heavy weights, because of the risk of soreness and stress in the joints.

Over a season, many performance skiers notice an increase in their anaerobic capacity but a decline in the aerobic. You may want to increase aerobic activity by using a stair climber or rowing machine, or by signing up for an aerobics class, which provides a lot of movement, too. If you can get in some basketball, volleyball, squash, or racquetball, you also will get a good endurance workout and emphasize coordination, speed, and quickness.

The Workout

It is important that any workout be interesting and challenging. This requires a lot of variety. There are enough exercises and variations that building in variety should be no problem.

Some exercises focus on agility and coordination, such as cone running; others emphasize strength and endurance, such as tuck jumps. A good workout includes exercises all along the spectrum. When planning a workout, consider at what point you introduce which activity. Balance exercises at the end of a hard workout won't do much for either your confidence or your skill, since fatigued muscles won't do what you want them to do.

Warm up, then stretch. Do balance and coordination exercises, such as standing on one leg with your eyes closed, or hoop running. Then do speed and quickness drills with cones, partners, or lines on a field. Now you can do more strength exercises, minute drills, or speed work on the track. Conclude with a cool-down and stretching.

As fatigue sets in, people start chatting and taking more time to move from one exercise to the next. Try to keep the momentum going by monitoring your pulse. Allow enough time between exercises for it to recover to an elevated but acceptable level—to 110, for example. For a hard ninety-second interval exercise, you may need two or three minutes of recovery before you repeat.

Emphasize technique and proper form. When you

Sample Microcycle

	Monday	Tuesday	Wednesday	Thursday	Friday	Saturday	Sunday
Active rest	Day off	In-line skate 1 hour	Swim 1 hour (A.M.) Run 45 minutes (P.M.)	Tennis 2 hours	Run 1 hour	Kayak 4 hours	Mountain bike 6 hours
Preparation	**Gym** Warm-up Stretch Bench press 4×20 Upright rows 4×20 Pec deck 4×15 Lat pull 4×20 Leg press 5×25 Leg curl 4×20 Thigh adductor 4×20 Abdominal routine	Run 45-minute fartlek Push-ups Sit-ups	**Gym** Warm-up Stretch Stair master 20 minutes Pull-ups/dips Pec deck 4×20 Lat pull 4×20 Leg extensions 4×15 Leg curls 4×15 Dead lift 4×20 Abdominal machine Stretch	Soccer 2 hours	**Gym** Warm-up Stretch Decline press 4×20 Upright rows 4×20 Flyes 4×15 Bent over rows 4×15 Curls 5×15 Triceps press 5×15 Straight-arm dumbbell raises 4×15 Squats 4×20 Standing leg curl 4×15 Stretch	Mountain bike 2 hours	Day off
Maximum strength	**Gym** Warm-up Stretch Bench press 4×8 Lat pull 3×10 Upright rows 3×10 Military press 3×8 Curls 4×10 Triceps press 3×10 Dumbbell pullover 3×10 Straight-arm raises 3×10 Leg extensions 3×8 Leg curls 3×8 Abdominal machine 3×10 Abdominal routine Stretch	**Dryland** Warm-up Stretch Ball drills 4×440s 4×100s Lunge jumps Lunge walk Girardellis Backward runs Abdominal routine Stretch	**Gym** Warm-up Stretch Stair master Bench press 4×8 Decline press 3×8 Pec deck 4×10 Bench curls 3×8 Triceps press 3×8 Leg extensions 4×10 Leg curls 3×8 Abdominal machine 3×10 Back extensions 2×20 Stretch	**Dryland** Warm-up Stretch Cone drills Hill sprints Shuttle runs Girardellis Backward runs Hopping Tuck jumps Box run Basketball Stretch	**Gym** Warm-up Stretch Bench press 3×8 Lat pull 3×10 Pec deck 4×10 Curls 3×10 Triceps press 3×10 Leg press 3×12 Squats 4×10 Leg extensions 3×10 Leg curls 3×10 Adductor machine 3×10 Abductor machine 3×10 Stretch	Mountain run 2 hours Stretch	Day off

	Day 1	Day 2	Day 3	Day 4	Day 5	Day 6	Day 7
Conversion	**Dryland** Warm-up Stretch Basketball Par course Dryland slalom Jump rope Hoop drills Tuck jumps Girardellis Abdominal routine Stretch	**Gym** Warm-up Stretch Bench press 3 × 12 Lat pull 3 × 15 Seated row 4 × 15 Dead lift 4 × 20 Leg press 5 × 15 Squats 4 × 15 Sport cord 5 × 15 Leg curls 4 × 12 Adductor machine 3 × 15 Back extensions 3 × 20 Abdominal routine	**Dryland** Warm-up Stretch Cone drills Minute drills Relay races Box course Stair runs Bench jumps Girardellis Lunge jumping Keep-away Stretch	**Gym** Warm-up Stretch Bench press 3 × 15 Lat pull 3 × 15 Upright row 3 × 15 Pec deck 4 × 15 Curls 3 × 15 Triceps press 3 × 15 Straight-arm raises 4 × 12 Leg press 4 × 20 Leg curls 4 × 12 Back extensions 3 × 20 Abdominal machine 4 × 15 Stretch	**Dryland** Warm-up Stretch Ball drills Balance drills 3 × 100s 5 × 40s Cariocas Girardellis Combination tuck drills Abdominal routine Stretch	In-line skate 1 hour Stretch	Day off Stretch
Maintenance	Day off Stretch	**Gym** Warm-up Stretch Stair master Bench press 3 × 15 Lat pull 3 × 12 Curls 3 × 12 Triceps press 3 × 15 Squats 4 × 15 Leg curls 3 × 12 Abdominal routine Stretch	Night skiing	**Club** Squash 1 hour Stretch Jacuzzi	**Home** Stretch Push-ups Sit-ups Sport cord Turbo trainer	Skiing Stretch	

try a new exercise that takes skill, walk through it first so you understand what moves are needed. For instance, if you are doing a relay and you must do several things before you cross the line, visualize the run before you start.

Sample Microcycle

The chart logs samples of strenuous weekly programs that you might undertake in each of the five periods. Any week would require a lot of energy and stamina, and reflects actual training log entries from several performance skiers. You may notice that within a cycle, sets and reps vary from one exercise to another. This is because the athlete may feel a little stronger in some exercises than others, he may have bitten off a little more than he could chew, or he just wanted some variety. Nevertheless, there is consistency within each workout compared with the volume and intensity of the succeeding cycle.

Though sets and reps for strength conditioning are indicated, the weight, obviously, is up to each individual. You can assume the athlete is working at the limit of endurance to complete the last few reps in the last sets. To help you figure a manageable load, six reps is equal to about 85% of your maximum, and ten reps is equivalent to approximately 70% of your maximum.

NINE

The Basic Turn

YIN—YANG. To excel at any sport, you must constantly resolve the opposites of complexity and simplicity. The expert skier skips and glides down the slope, flowing like water over a streambed, with suppleness and economy of movement. It appears so extraordinarily simple . . .

At the upper end, a skier may say he is doing nothing more than a combination of a few simple steps: moving up and down, back and forth, and twisting around his long axis. Horst Abraham, a developer of U.S. teaching methodology, said, "Skiing can be viewed as a composite of many hundreds of skills or it can be seen as just one: balance in motion."

Skiing makes a visceral connection not with the intellect, but with the part of the brain that deals with movement and feelings. Modern equipment is more responsive than ever, so the expert skier seems to do more with far fewer overt movements. Lower-level learning concerns distinct motor movements; upper-level questions are more apt to deal with feeling: "Where do you feel the pressure in your foot?" "Do you feel stable with your weight on one foot?"

If skiing were simple, everyone would perform at a

high level—or no one would, because it would be boring. As in most skill sports, there are thousands of minute corrections in body angle and attitude during a run.

It's easy to walk down a sidewalk; try to do the same thing on the rail of a train track. The interesting thing is that with practice, you can soon lope down a rail with confidence. Practice develops kinesthetic awareness—your sense of movement and position in space. At first you bumble along, then you learn to make many tiny corrections quickly and early, but more important, subconsciously.

Skiing is really pretty simple in terms of basic movements, but becoming coordinated and efficient comes only from many hours on the hill. You develop a range of movement and timing consistent with your speed and conditions. Gradually, these become instinctive and reflexive.

What is so marvelous about the nervous system is its adaptability. The brain does not generate preprogrammed body movement; it adjusts and modifies movement based on changing information it receives. A robot arm can be programmed to pour a cup of coffee, but move the cup, and you've got a mess. A skier can spend a lot of time training to make a great turn on hard snow, yet with just a little attention to feelings, he can quickly modify his technique to handle wet snow through the trees.

For beginners, everything is new and the emphasis is on developing correct movements. At the intermediate level, prominent or awkward movements may be stilled. At the expert level, considerable energy and concentration are required to make even the smallest gains. The difference between an excellent and a marginal day often comes down to attitude. If you are enervated and vigorous, you can take your skills to the limit. When you are apathetic or distracted, your skiing can regress several years.

Two strategies to help you progress from one level to the next are to review the basics and to try some skill drills. You'll find that some of the on-snow drills help move you along. The most important thing is to ensure you have a clear idea of technically correct skiing.

Utopian Skiing

The most difficult students are those who began without lessons, have been skiing for some time, and whose nervous systems are "hard-wired" on how to ski. This is all the more difficult because correct skiing isn't instinctive. A new skier on dizzying slopes instinctively wants to lean into the hill, to counter the speed by trying to get as far into the back seat as possible. To turn, he tries to throw his upper body around to make the skis go the same way. Performance skiers try to find the optimum body position needed to balance all the forces while letting the skis run to the limit of their capability under any given conditions. While there is a "correct" way to ski, the expert skier modifies his basic movements with a variety of moves.

Like a jockey trying to get the most out of a horse, the expert skier feels for the "sweet spot" underfoot. His feet are sensitive to the rigidity of the skis, their turning radius, stability, and "snappiness." The mechanics of a turn also have to be adapted to match the performance of the skis.

Instructors usually look from the ground up to evaluate technique. If the skis are carving or skidding, instructors work up the body to see what is going on. I'm not going to try to describe or define turns for every situation, but by understanding one ideal turn, you can modify your moves to adapt to most conditions.

The principles of ergonomic skiing apply whether you are a racer or prefer slower, more stylish skiing. They involve framing your position to emphasize skeletal strength.

Carving and the Turn Shape

In a medium- to long-radius turn, movements are slower and you have more time to think than in short fall-line turns. Despite the simple movements, longer turns also are technically more difficult. Why? Because short turns involve more skidding or pivoting. Anyone can skid; the long turn relies on a carving ski.

In the carved turn, the ski has to be rolled up on its edge and bent into reverse camber by applied pressure. Just like a cyclist guiding a bicycle through a turn, the skier has to find the balance point. If all points on the edge pass through the same point in a

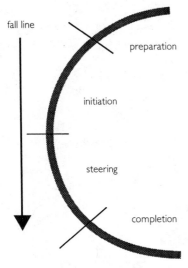

The four-phase turn model illustrates where specific actions take place. **Preparation:** *upper body faces downhill, torso muscles tense.* **Initiation:** *pole plant establishes platform, upper body moves across skis, weight is committed to outside ski as outside leg extends, skis' edge angle increases to build pressure, ski lead changes.* **Steering:** *body sinks and hips angulate to control edge angle and pressure on skis.* **Completion:** *pressure shifts toward skis' tails, feet move directly beneath hips.*

turn, the ski is carving. Performance skis are very sensitive to this and react quickly, but carving continuous high-speed turns smoothly across the hill, without slipping or chattering, is still an art.

The four-phase turn model involves preparation, initiation, steering, and completion. (This model helps describe where things happen, but we are more concerned with how things happen.) Some experts have abbreviated the four-phase concept to two: turn initiation, which involves unweighting, transferring the weight, pivoting, and edging; and turn completion, composed of balancing against the ski as it moves through the turn. This model immediately addresses the key concern of the performance skier: carving control throughout the turn. The two-phase model emphasizes movements at the top of the turn.

Unlike a car, whose turning radius can vary by steering, a carved ski has a fixed turning radius. To turn inside this, some skidding or pivoting is inevitable, forcing the shape out of a half-circle. Often, snow tracks look like commas or fishhooks. Why is that important? For many, the hardest part of the turn is at the end of the arc, when centrifugal force and gravity push the skier out of the path of the turn. If the forces are too much for the edge to hold its line, the ski moves sideways, chatters, skids, and loses speed. The skier no longer has a stable base. Many skiers try to figure out how to counter these strong forces at the end of the turn. Some try to strengthen their legs, which helps. Others file their edges razor-sharp, which also works. It's often better to look at how you set up coming into the turn, however.

If you flatten, pivot, or steer the skis, accelerate through the fall line, then apply strong edge and pressure at the end, your radius will be longer at the top (the first phase) and shorter through the second. The speed gained at the top generates a lot of centrifugal force as the arc tightens up. If speed is high enough or the slope is steep or the snow is hard, you may not hold the edge however much pressure you apply.

Rolling the edge over high in the turn, where centrifugal force is low, and getting an edge early in the turn are the secrets to managing these forces and maintaining momentum into the next turn. The dif-

Former member of the U.S. Ski Team Tracy McEwan shows that a classic carved turn can be relaxed yet aggressive. With arms comfortably apart and forward for improved balance, she drops her hips toward the inside of the turn to roll her skis up on edge. Her outside knee is bent but not twisted.

Executing a strong lead change, her shoulders, hips, knees, and feet have all been shifted equally. She drops her hips, maintains a rounded back, and centers her weight over the sweet spot of the ski.

With her hips directly over her bindings, McEwan shifts her weight onto her new outside (right) ski. She can now steer with subtle foot pressure and pole plant with a flick of her wrist.

Even as her upper body leans toward the inside of the turn, she makes another lead change with her shoulders and hips. With her weight mostly on the outside ski, she begins to drop her hips to generate good edge hold.

ference between round (or C-) turns and J-turns is that J-turns can work well for strong skiers at low speeds, but even elite skiers edge early to make a C-shape in long, high-speed turns.

C-turns are not always best. Skiing steep slopes or powder often calls for a J-turn path. The tightened radius at the end allows the skis to sink deep and set hard. The hard set can cut your speed, but the increased energy down on the ski allows you to either pop out of deep snow or clear the ground so that tips and tails can change direction on the steep.

Think about different turn shapes when considering how to get the skis into and out of the turn.

Dryland Turn Mechanics

Let's try skiing on the floor where we can break the movement into segments without being on skis. Think about how you move in relation to the skis. This is easily done in a six-foot-wide hallway so that you can balance yourself against the walls.

First, understand your center of mass or center of gravity. This is your central point of balance. If you attached a light to the outside of a ball and rolled it down a hill, the point of light would make loops. If the ball were transparent and the light were suspended inside at its center, the point of light would travel in a straight line. Skiers have a center, and since they move around on changing terrain, this central balance point moves around. If you ski smoothly without thrashing, it's easier to move your center to anticipate speed, terrain, and direction changes. If you move your center erratically or don't make corrective moves, you will fall over. Your center is normally at about 55% of your height, two inches or so below the navel and halfway inside through the body. It is lower when you're wearing skis and boots, at about 45% of your height.

Imagine you have just finished a turn to your right and are going to move into another from the traverse. Stand in the middle of the hall. Your feet should be comfortably spaced, about shoulder-width apart, and your right foot ahead of the left by about a half-foot length. Place your right hand on the near wall, keeping your head and back upright and slightly curved, and shoulders level. Now bend at the knees and move your hips in toward the wall. By bracing your arm against the wall, you can bring your center over the black spot in the diagram's lower right quadrant. In skiing, you have the back of the boots to press against. Keep your knees bent forward so that they are over your toes, not your heels. For a moment, put all your weight on the left foot. Call this the finished position of your previous turn. Go through the numbers.

1. Up-unweight. Coming from a compressed position, stand up. Your center will now move from down and back of center to up and over your feet in the middle of the circle. Do this not by pushing off the wall with your hand, but by stepping down with your right foot. As you stand directly over your feet, you'll notice that they are flat on the floor. On snow, the skis will be flat, too.

2. Move forward and inside. From your initial position, your center continues to move forward, so you feel your weight move onto the balls of your toes and also to your left (or the inside of the new turn).

While you move up and forward, shuffle your left foot forward so that the toe of your left foot is ahead of the right foot, again by about a half-foot length.

As you start to fall to your left, change hands so that you now balance off the other wall. Again, keep your shoulders level. Your center is now over position three

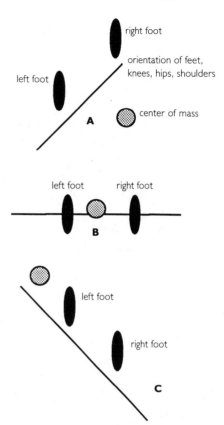

While practicing dryland turns, your center of mass should move from behind your right shoulder (A), through your feet (B), to in front of your left shoulder (C). Keep your body aligned and facing away from the near wall.

in the upper left quadrant. As you move to the inside, you'll notice pressure on the left edges of your feet.

3. *Drop the weight.* Now bend the knees and sink down with your buttocks. Do this slowly and notice the position of your hips as you sink down. If you made the above lead change, your hips will naturally be facing out toward the upper-right quadrant, depending on how much change you made. For the sake of this demonstration, relax your shoulders so that they fall in line with your hips, and you will be in the ideal counterrotated position.

Experiment in this position. Vary the relative angle by turning your shoulders clockwise or counterclockwise without changing your foot lead. If you are leaning in to your left, by moving clockwise with the shoulders, you increase the angle of your hips in the same direction, as well as the distance that your center can move to the inside.

Now try the counterclockwise position. Your hips want to open up more in the same direction as your feet, and your lead change will begin to diminish. You will also notice the tendency for your right heel to push out and away. These are all no-nos for the performance skier, and among the hardest faults to correct. By rotating any portion of your upper body in the same direction as the turn, you lose the strong balance position on your skis, and the tail of your downhill ski will skid. It also takes some effort to overrotate or underrotate your upper body relative to the position of your feet, knees, and hips.

Repeat this exercise in the opposite manner as if you were going to turn to the right. This is a simple little exercise, but it is a good one, especially when done in front of a full-length mirror. The point is that when moving from one turn to the next, you want to project your center of mass from the tails of your skis, first up over the bindings, then forward and to the inside of the new turn. With nothing more than this simple up-forward-down, accompanied by a realignment along the diagonal of feet, knees, hips, and shoulder, you've made the basic moves of the world's best skiers—and how much energy did it take?

Of course, on snow, it's a bit more challenging. It's

hard to maintain a good countered position as you run across the hill. Regardless of how efficient you are, at medium to high speeds with precise carving arcs, there will be stress in your quadriceps that you must strongly resist. The hardest thing about making good turns may be just trying to hang on through the last third. Rick Reid, a Pacific Northwest coach who occasionally works with the U.S. Ski Team, commented, "The reason Tomba and Girardelli hold a countered position so well across the hill is because they're built like Coke machines."

Another obvious difference is that it's one thing to assume an upright, balanced position in your hallway and another to do the same on a sloping hill. To keep even pressure on the ski, your stance has to be perpendicular to the skis, not the horizon. On flatter slopes, this isn't a problem, but as the hill gets steeper, you really have to project your body forward with the same effort made by a sprinter coming out of the blocks or a gymnast lunging into the vault. Many skiers try to bend in the knees and waist, but don't think about their ankles. Bending at the knees without flexing in the ankles simply drops your rear end. To counter the rearward shift in the center of mass, the reflexive response then is to bend at the waist. In this position, the skier is structurally weak, with little ability to absorb shocks.

As was suggested in the dryland exercise, when you cross the center over the skis, there is a strong forward movement, hinged at the ankles. This movement maintains the upper body's perpendicularity to the skis. Should feet be together or apart? If you're not into racing, beauty is in the eye of the beholder. If you like speed, a wide stance is preferable because of its greater base of support. Also, whenever feet come together, the legs tend to flex and extend simultaneously. Imagine riding in a car whose rear wheels are locked together.

Spin-offs and Spinouts

Once you feel the flow of this technique, you will discover that the more aggressively you project your mass forward and in, the farther you extend your legs away from your center. While the knee should still be bent forward, the leg will be virtually in line from the foot to the hip along its long axis. This is an extremely strong position; as centrifugal force and gravity combine, the pressure you feel on your ski through your leg can be countered by the inherent strength of the skeletal structure. As the skier crosses the fall line at the end of a turn, he can absorb bumpy terrain by flexing in the knee and ankle.

Knees are not designed to bend sideways when you are standing erect. What is usually called knee angulation is a combination of inward rotation of the femur in the hip socket and normal in-line knee flexion while the hips remain up over the feet. With excessive knee angulation, as the leg retracts and extends to absorb terrain, the lateral angle formed at the knee by the thigh and calf has to be moved in and out. This causes the ski to roll on and off the edge, alternately grabbing and slipping throughout the arc of a long turn.

For fast, short fall-line turns, keep the hips up over the skis and cross over the skis, emphasizing knee angulation. This has been calculated at as many as two to two and a half turns per second. In a long turn, it is difficult to develop strong edge pressure on the ski without angulation in the hip. When you align your center of mass through your ankle to the outside edge, you are in the edging position for any degree of angulation. If your center is misaligned outward, the skis will flatten. If you are misaligned inward, your weight will shift onto the inside ski.

You must hold more edge angle as centrifugal forces increase. This requires hip movement inward to keep the center-ankle-edge alignment. Too much edge angle for your speed and the ski won't decamber and arc. As you refine your turn by moving forward and in, you may also discover unwanted banking or inward leaning at the end of your turn. As you extend to move out of the previous turn, your body comes out of a crouch and straightens. If you hold your upper and lower body in rigid alignment as you settle into the new turn, you will quickly face these problems. Without extending your upper body out over the hill as the skis come out of the fall line and into the traverse, your weight remains on the inside ski, and the downhill ski loses edge contact and slips. You either slide down on your hip or ride off across the hill, caught on your uphill ski. If this occurs, you may be moving your center sideways across the skis without coming forward as well. Also, concentrate on leveling your shoulders throughout the turn, which requires loose hips. Think about driving the outside hand down and to the outside as well.

Because the back is supple and can twist without limiting forward and backward flexion, the upper body can continue to face downhill and extend out over the downhill ski through the last part of the turn. Many skiers have trouble holding a good line on steep hills and hard snow. They swing the outside arm toward the tip of the skis through the last third of the turn in anticipation of the pole plant. This arm swing causes the shoulders and hips to square up in the direction of travel of the skis. When the hips square up, they move back in over the feet, reducing the edge angle. Without good edge angle and pressure, the skis chatter and slip.

Inward lean engages the edge of your ski higher at the top of your turn, allowing smooth and progressive pressure. Again, through the top of the turn, your legs are away from you and you are leaning toward the center of the new turn. This puts the skis on edge right at the top of the arc. This is very effective on hard snow. By letting the pressure on the ski build smoothly and gradually throughout the crux of the turn, you have greater control.

If you have to stomp on the ski as it comes out of the fall line to hold its arc, the edge is much more likely to chatter and bounce. Additionally, you've put all your energy into that short impulse. If you set your ski too hard and quickly, you will tend to rebound. This is the cue for the ski to initiate a direction change, probably earlier than you want.

Rites of Initiation

We've been discussing body movement and angles. Now let's look below your feet at the characteristics of the skis. The next time you're on the hill, try the world's simplest turn. Find a smooth slope of moderate pitch. Stand with your skis perpendicular to the fall line. You should have to set your edges to hold by angulating slightly. Turn your upper body so it faces squarely downhill with your hands about chest high. Because your knees are angled into the hill, they are also bent. Stay relaxed, stand up, and go with whatever happens.

The skis begin to sideslip. Quickly, the tips drop and the skis run downhill. You've actually loaded a lot of potential energy into the system by facing downhill with your upper body. To see how much, stand up, keep your feet planted, twist your torso as far as you can, and see how long you can hold this position.

Remember the Slinky? It was a spring toy that flip-flopped down the stairs. If you held the Slinky at the bottom, twisted the top, and released the bottom, it uncoiled in the same direction as the twist. On skis, you release the spring by reducing the edge angle and flattening the skis out. The preturn upper-body twist is also known as anticipation.

Repeat this experiment with different degrees of anticipation. You will discover that tuned skis need little impetus to turn from a traverse across the fall line. The quicker you want to come around, the more upper-body anticipation you will need.

In quick, short-radius turns where centrifugal forces are not high, the skier can keep the hips over the feet. The upper body faces down the hill through all phases of the turn, and given the tight arc that the skis follow, the upper and lower body can be twisted in opposition to each other, almost to the limit of the skier's flexibility. When you release the edge and let the body unwind, the skis come back around in the new direction. By planting the pole solidly, you can anchor your upper body so that all the unwinding energy goes toward changing the direction of the skis. This is another argument for having a strong upper body.

Twisting the upper and lower body into an anticipated position does not really require great muscular effort. The skis are moving faster than your body. Their speed and direction naturally put a lot of torque into your midsection. Rather than try to twist away so as to face squarely downhill, try to maintain a balanced position with your upper body facing downhill. On moguls particularly, think of having a swivel joint in the hips.

Because tuned skis readily want to change direction

from the traverse into the fall line, turn initiation is fairly straightforward. If you feel you are not entering your turn smoothly or quickly enough, put more unwinding energy into the system by increasing your upper-body anticipation with head and shoulders more squarely downhill. Also, flatten the skis by standing taller at the start of the turn (up-unweighting) or sinking faster by totally relaxing your hips and thighs (down-unweighting).

Pressure Cooking

So, which ski do you pressure? The answer depends on your disposition, turning radius, speed, conditions, and slope of the hill. You will want to finish each turn with most of your weight squarely on the downhill or outside leg. Without too much trouble, you can turn on your inside ski, but your body as a unit develops much more mechanical stability braced against the outside foot.

Stylish skiers often make an imperceptible weight transfer from one foot to the other, but a minimal weight shift that retains much weight on the inside ski will not decamber or bend the outside ski necessary for carving. This confines your skis to only modest direction changes out of the fall line unless they rattle off into a loose long-radius turn. To arc strongly out of the fall line or to hold on hard snow, the performance skier commits his weight predominantly over the outside ski.

When you were learning to walk, you deliberately picked up one foot, put it down, and got your balance all over again. It's the same in skiing. The equivalent here means picking up your inside foot to ensure no weight is on it as you arc through the finish of one turn, then quite deliberately putting it back on the snow and standing on it—now the new outside ski—as you balance your way through the next turn.

The problem with discussing skiing technique is that on the hill, movement is continuous. To examine it, it has to be broken up into still fragments. This may cause people to focus too closely on one part. During the early 1970s, Patrick Russel was one of the finest slalom skiers in the world. Photographs of him showed pronounced downward movement onto the tails of his skis at the end of a turn. A generation of young racers took this and blew it all out of proportion. Jet- and Cheetah-Stix—add-on plastic supports for the back of boots—sold like hotcakes as kids flew down the hill sitting back on the tails of their skis. It was fast in a straight line, but no one could turn very well. Ignored was the fact that Russel was incredibly fit and could get quite low on his skis, but he also had a strong up-and-forward movement coming into a new turn.

It's common to get wrapped up in one technical aspect of skiing and then overlook others. Keep the big picture in mind.

TEN

Skiing Drills on Your Own

THIS CHAPTER PRESENTS exercises that coaches and instructors use to focus on different skills. All are relatively simple. Take a couple up to the hill and try them when things are slow.

U.S. Ski Team member Hillary Lindh believes that drills don't need to be complicated: "They can be developed from any little part of your skiing. You can concentrate on turning with all your weight on your outside ski, for example. There. You've just done a drill."

To improve your performance, you must be adaptable. To break out of a conditioned set of responses, experiment with new forces, angles, and movements. Exercises are one approach to learning; another good way to improve is to ski with others better than you are. Some people learn by listening, some by seeing, and others by doing. When you ski with someone with better skills, you can do all three. Ask questions on the lift, watch your buddy, pick out something, and try to emulate it.

The performance skier seeks mastery by being the eternal student. He listens to what others have to say, takes what works, and leaves the rest. There are lots of fine skiers whose every turn looks like the last. The performance skier likes to experiment. He establishes a performance envelope with minimums and maximums in which he knows he can operate, and always looks to push the limits. You can take any of the suggestions that follow and test their limits. You may fall a few times, but then you'll better understand what works and what doesn't.

Postural Drills

Pelvic tilt. Stand with your feet comfortably four to six inches apart. Start with your head. Remember the hula dancer with the bobbing head you see in the rear window of cars? Imagine this is your head and it's balanced comfortably on top of your shoulders. If you totally relax your neck muscles, it's not going to slide off. Raise your arms and roll your shoulders forward slightly. Round your back and bend the knees and ankles. Now roll the bottom of your pelvis forward and back. If you concentrate, you should feel a hinging in the lower back. When the bottom of your pelvis is back (your rear end is slightly sticking out), you are in a weak skiing position. A duck would ski this way. When it is forward, you are in a strong position, with natural round curves along your spine. Remember, especially when skiing over rough terrain, keep the back round by tilting the pelvis forward.

Fore and aft position. Lean from the ankles forward in a traverse, first putting pressure on the tips, then back, pressuring the tails. Do the same while variously bending your knees as well. Think about how well the tip initiates into a turn. Feel how the tail holds through the end of a turn. This exercise may be nothing more than feeling weight up on your toes or resting on top of your heels.

The Wedge and Wedge Christie

Everyone who began in ski school remembers the wedge turn. If you're older, you probably remember it as the more embarrassing snowplow. Regardless of terminology, many advanced skiers feel that it has little relevance to them now other than as a way to slow down when entering the lift line. Try wedge turning again for a few moments. It provides good feedback on several fundamentals.

Without skis, stand, spread your legs, and turn your toes in and heels out. You will feel your balance point move back so that if your knees or ankles remained unbent (or you don't break at the waist), you will fall over. Proper wedge maneuvers at any speed also take leg strength. Skis in the wedge position expose more surface to the snow. Weak beginners will start downhill in a wedge, pick up speed as the angle is forced closed, and ultimately career out of control. They will first instinctively lock their knees to resist this closing movement, then bend at the waist to keep their weight forward. In this position, they've corrected two problems only to generate more interesting ones.

Wedge turns can be made by gentle steering or rotation of the outside leg and foot, or with a carving action by displacing more weight over the outside ski and pressing the knee forward and in. Do some wedge turns and really concentrate on differentiating between these methods. Which do you prefer and why? When skiing parallel at faster speeds, you may not be aware of the differences between sliding and edging.

If you are a strong skier, wedge turning can be almost too simple. With a nice, light touch on your edges, you can initiate a wedge or even a simple parallel christie with almost no discernible body movement. An observer may think that you are simply finessing your ankles to turn and following your skis around with few, if any, apparent body angles other than wedged skis. Because wedge maneuvers are frequently performed at slower-than-normal speed, very good skiers often rotate their outside hip around, which they would never do at cruising speeds. Feel comfortable making slow wedge turns with good countering while moving the hip to the inside.

It's also not as easy as it seems to make good wedge turns while maintaining a little natural arm carriage and swing. When instructors wedge around, they sometimes look like they forgot to take the hanger out of their parka. Challenge yourself and ask, "How slow can I go and still make a good flowing turn?"

At higher speeds, carving turns in a NASTAR-type (read "lots of turns") slalom course while holding a solid wedge throughout quickly develops good weight transfer and angulation skills. These are flip sides of a coin. You can't do either without really moving your upper body out over the downhill ski on each turn. If your ski tips cross momentarily while you are doing this exercise, you have not completely transferred your weight to the outside ski. If the tail of your inside ski drags, you are back on your heels. Move your center of mass forward onto your toes.

Using the wedge turn between parallel ski traverses is known as the wedge christie. These turns help teach you how to move dynamically toward the inside of your turn. Because you move your uphill leg away from you slightly uphill, the moment you pick up your downhill ski to match your outside ski in a parallel fashion, you have removed your base of support from directly underneath you. Your center of mass will be to the inside of your skis and toward the origin of the turning radius. Your skis will immediately be on edge because of your inward lean. See how far you can flare your outside ski and thereby how far you can displace your center and still turn effectively.

An effective wedge christie polished up on easier runs is indispensable for the performance skier on very steep slopes. There, you settle into each turn in a crouched position with your skis near or perpendicular to the fall line for optimum edge hold. For control, above all, keep your speed consistent. By releasing your edges and letting the skis simply drop into the fall line, chances are you will accelerate far quicker than you want, making a controlled follow-on edge set shaky at best. Even if you do contain this speed by slamming on your edges, the rebound may be more than you bargained for. By stemming the uphill ski out of one turn, you can transfer your weight quickly and eliminate much of the slide-and-glide phase between turns. By reducing the time the skis are dropping in the fall line, you keep acceleration and deceleration closer together while increasing the tempo of your edge sets. If the tail of your uphill ski drags on the snow, get more of your weight up on your toes or simply lift your heel when you flare the ski out.

Pole Drills

Pole use is one of the stylized aspects of your skiing. You often can recognize someone from a distance by their style, particularly the way they carry their arms and the swing of the poles. Poles help establish a strong platform from which to unweight and move into turns.

Balance bar. The moment the pole is planted is a signal to the body to move. Imagine your poles as the ends of a long balance beam. Extend your arms forward and to the sides, then cock your wrists slightly forward. The poles flare out, substantially increasing the inertial resistance to torque in your upper body. At high speeds and in long turns, a wide arm and pole position will help you establish a rock-steady upper body.

Cat whiskers. A less appreciated function of poles is to provide a sense of the slope. Let the basket brush (as opposed to drag) against the snow on your uphill side. From time to time, focus on your pole grip on that side. Your vision, focused down the hill, and your touch, focused up the hill, expand your awareness. It may not be apparent at first, but gradually you will appreciate the bit of additional information from your hands.

The no-pole plant. As your speed increases and turning radius becomes longer, pole plants are less important. Actually, planting the pole sends too much of a quick shock through your upper body. It is more important to concentrate on slower, more flowing movement at such times. Pole plants always make sense during short, quick turns and on steeper slopes. Make some long turns without planting your poles, then start shortening the radius to determine when the plant becomes important again.

Handlebar drill. A somewhat overrated exercise is to take your poles off your wrists, place them together, and grasp the shafts as you would a mountain bike's handlebars. Now your hands work together instead of independently. The idea is to hold the poles steady as you turn while facing squarely downhill. This will keep you from swinging your arms around excessively and quiets your upper body.

The airplane variation. If you've got this exercise down pat, try a variation: Hold your poles as you normally would, with your hands in front. Then make everything rigid from your shoulders down and turn your elbows out so the top of your grips face each other. The baskets should be level with your chest and in line with your hands. Imagine your poles are wings and you must keep them straight and level. Of course, you will look like an idiot, but make a series of medium-radius turns.

When you hold your poles out in this exercise, you will be able to see how still your hands are by watching the pole baskets with your peripheral vision. Done correctly, this exercise is difficult. You can get somewhat the same effect with a bamboo slalom pole, but when the slope becomes steeper, the pole will usually bury an end in the hill.

Double outside pole plant. This plant to the downhill side is a great way to work on your upper body position. Make a series of short- to medium-radius turns. At the plant, touch both pole tips down the hill. This is awkward at first, but after a few times, you will see how it can make you square your upper body down the hill. It also eliminates any dropping of the outside arm.

Wrist flick plant. Some skiers have a fairly elaborate pole plant. From somewhere around their back pocket, they may swing the arm up, pull their elbows in, cock the wrist, drop the arm, and stab the ground. To lose some excess motion, stand erect with your hands forward and poles hanging from your hands

Although the double outside pole plant is a simple drill, it will really help you keep your shoulders square and facing downhill.

with their tips about four inches off the ground. Swing a pole forward by cocking only the wrist. Don't move anything else. Now, bend in the knees. Voilà! The pole is planted. Try making short turns, setting the pole only with wrist-and-bends. Once you have a good rhythm, gradually flex your arms and shoulders more so that you are not so stiff.

Weight Transfer Drills

Refer to the diagram of the four phases of the turn mentioned in the previous chapter. The phase two zone is usually when you want to begin shifting weight and applying pressure to the outside ski. That's not gospel, because the timing depends on the situation. Develop your moves and enhance your awareness by experimenting with different weight transfer points around the arc of the turn. Try these exercises on a smooth slope while making medium to long turns.

Late transfer. Transfer your weight and pressure the ski at a point all the way down in the early phase four zone. Start with the skiddiest version. As you finish one turn, extend upward to flatten the skis, then just use your anticipated position and a little foot steering to point the tips down the fall line and drift into the turn. Be sure to extend at an angle, no more than perpendicular to the slope. Tipping too far to the inside of the turn will edge the skis. Keep the skis as flat as possible until you come out of the fall line, where keeping a flat ski will cause a sideslip. As you come out of the fall line, come down solidly on the outside ski so you have good edge bite. Link several of these skidded turns together.

Transfer in the fall line. Repeat the above maneuver, but when the flat skis drift into the fall line, lift the inside ski and drop your rear end so your weight settles onto the outside ski. Timing is important in order to transfer your weight from the inside ski to the outside ski and to start to edge just as you are parallel with the fall line.

Early transfer. This time, transfer your weight onto an edge before you drop into the fall line, at a point associated with phase one. Exaggerate your transfer by traversing across the hill with a raised uphill ski.

Keep your upper body squarely down the hill. Now, step down solidly with the uphill ski, lift your inside ski, flex forward in your ankles, and tip your upper body forward and toward the center of the turn. These moves will put you on the inside edge of the outside ski before you enter the fall line. As you turn, increase the edge angle with a continuous sinking motion.

Squaring Drills

Keeping the upper body facing squarely downhill provides potential energy for unwinding the skis in a new direction and allows the hips to move to the inside of the turn for angulation.

Javelin turn. Popularized by 1970s trick skier Art Furrer, the javelin turn forces the upper body to align square to the fall line by advancing your uphill hip. From a traverse, pick up your uphill ski and swing the tip across your downhill ski, a few inches above it. As you improve, try to make crossing of the skis a natural movement done right at the moment of weight transfer. This way, you have a little centrifugal force against which you can balance. Like many other drills, this only helps if you remember what your hip and shoulder position was once you go back to normal turning.

Hand drop. As you make your usual long turn, instead of keeping both hands forward, allow your downhill outside arm to hang back so that a line from your hand down to your ski would fall behind your heel

The javelin turn, or X-turn, develops independent leg action and reinforces proper hip and shoulder position. To get a feel for the body position taught with this drill, stand without skis and cross one leg in front of the other.

The hand-drop exercise will help eliminate the common problem of upper-body over-rotation. Initiate a turn as usual with an inside-arm pole plant, but concentrate on dropping your outside arm behind your hips.

binding. This will keep your shoulders from rotating with the skis. Remember, this is only an exercise. Don't let dropping your hand become part of your regular technique.

Double pole plant. Many racers make a simultaneous double pole plant. This may not be the most elegant skiing, but it provides great stability. It also has much the same effect as the hand drop drill but affects the other side of your body. A double pole plant forces the uphill shoulder and arm forward and avoids the whammy of dropping the inside arm down and back, which causes leaning in and rotation.

Hat trick. Lloyd Scroggins, assistant coach at Crystal Mountain, Washington, developed this one. It's best if you're wearing a cowboy hat or baseball cap. Ski down the fall line at a good clip, take your hat off, and place it on your chest. If your upper body always faces your direction of travel, the wind will keep it plastered on your chest. As soon as your upper body rotates away from this direction, the wind will push it off.

The backward drill. This can instill all the wrong ideas, but I include it because it worked well for me once when I was grappling with overrotation. Make sure you have a lot of hill from side to side. Start with a normal, shallow-angle traverse. As you slide across the hill, advance your downhill foot, knee, hip, shoulder, and arm forward so that your upper body is facing squarely uphill. If your balance is good, you up-unweight strongly, and you move to the inside of the turn while transferring your weight onto your new outside ski, you can turn in this manner. Making such giant lead changes before you enter the fall line will guarantee that you complete the turn in a strongly countered square position down the hill. Link a few of these together.

Why do some coaches hate this exercise? Normally you would want your upper body facing downhill; in this exercise it faces uphill, as if overrotated. Try to make complete lead changes so your downhill ski, knee, hip, and shoulder are simultaneously ahead in the traverse. In any case, if you don't like it, don't do it.

One-Ski Turns

At my home area in Washington, the juniors of the Crystal Mountain Alpine Club practice on one ski to develop balance, coordination, and strength. It also teaches them to commit into the new turn. Because almost everyone has a dominant leg, it's usually easier to do on one than the other.

One ski unweighted. You don't have to leave one ski parked at the top to practice this. Link a series of turns on one ski only. You'll get better balance by

One-ski turns develop the ambidexterity necessary for performance skiing. White Pass Ski Team assistant coach Lloyd Scroggins presses his knees together to prevent his free leg from swinging around and altering his balance.

Rick Reid, head coach of the Crystal Mountain Alpine Club, begins a hanger by completely unweighting his uphill ski. He gradually shifts his weight onto his outside ski—some as he enters the fall line and the rest as he finishes the turn.

pressing your knees together and letting the un-weighted ski angle away as if you were doing the Charleston.

Hangers. This turn is initiated by leaning to the inside as normal, but instead of transferring weight to the outside ski early, pressure and turn on the inside one. Step off onto the outside ski once you are parallel with or just coming out of the fall line into the completion part of the turn, and finish as you would any turn.

Reid is well-balanced as he performs an inside ski turn. Try combining a series of these maneuvers with a series of hangers to really develop your timing and weight shift.

In performing an outside ski turn, Lloyd Scroggins strongly commits his body over his skis and down the hill.

Inside ski turns. Make a left turn on your left ski, then a right turn on your right. Make complete turns always on the outside edge of the inside ski. This is completely contrary to what you normally do.

Edging Drills

Performance skiers are sensitive to the edges. Knowing precisely how much edge you need or want takes lots of practice in different conditions.

Edging in the traverse. Ski across the hill in a shallow traverse, increasing or decreasing edge angle. Get the ski to alternately slip and hold throughout the traverse. While it's slipping, don't let tips or tails slide lower than the other.

Full gliding spin. Ski down a smooth, flat slope, using a lot of up-unweighting. Let the skis get flat, twist your arms around in the direction you want to go, and try to spin your skis 360 degrees. This takes a little alternating edge angle, depending on where you are in the spin.

Hockey stop. On a slope of gentle to moderate pitch, ski straight down the fall line in a low body position with feet four to six inches apart. At some point, up-unweight strongly enough so you can pivot your skis ninety degrees to your direction of travel using your feet and knees. Keep your upper body facing downhill. Because of your speed and the suddenness of the skis' direction change, you will move into a moderate to

A controlled hockey stop requires fine edge control and independent movement of the upper and lower body. Practice coming to a stop at a line between two stationary poles with your hands and shoulders facing downhill.

quick sideslip. Look back up the hill. Your tracks should not wander over the hill.

Add the challenge of deceleratng through your side-slip so that you stop smoothly at a certain point on the slope. This means gradually increasing your edge angle. Plant your pole right at the full stop line. Be certain you have good control; otherwise, you may slide right up onto your pole shaft, which will stop your skis and flip you to the ground. Another variation is to set two poles about one and a half ski lengths apart, perpendicular to the fall line. Direct your side-slip through them. Master the fall-line hockey stop, then try the exercises again, this time slightly diag-onal to the fall line. Again, don't let the sideslip wander over the hill.

Angulation Drills

Your proficiency is partly defined by the range of angles you can achieve between upper and lower body while staying stable. The faster you carve a ski for any turning radius, the more edge angle you need to hold your line. The more edge angle there is, the more you have to balance laterally against the ski. Your balance is largely controlled by the kinds of angles your body makes.

Inclination drill. This enhances your balance by getting edge angle only through inclination, or total body angulation. You have a much smaller margin for balance errors without the use of your hips or knees. Inclined turns are made just as you would lean a bicycle through a turn. Anything other than a short fall-line turn will involve some inclination as you cross over the skis, but keep a straight, relaxed body in a countered position throughout the entire turn—no knee or hip angulation. Pretend you're surfing. To move from one turn to the next, reduce inclination by relaxing your legs and settling onto the skis. Centrifugal force will bring your hips back up over the skis if you have judged your speed and turning radius correctly.

This is fun, but if you turn like this consistently, it will catch up with you. Without at least leveling the shoulders or putting some soft curl into your body, you will do lots of hip checks and worse into the snow.

Hip angulation exercise. This is fairly standard when done with knee angulation, but is a more delicate balancing act done with hip angulation. At the top of a long, smooth pitch, ski diagonally down the hill, well-countered, with your weight over the downhill ski. During the traverse, get the ski to grip and ride the edge by dropping your hips into the hill, then alternately let the skis flatten and slip by raising your hips back over your boots. Keep your upper body facing squarely downhill throughout.

Knee angulation exercise. Knee angulation is actually a combination of inward rotation of the femur in the hip socket and a bending of the knee. Make some short turns with your hips over your feet. At each turn, reach down with your outside hand and place it on the side of your knee, consciously feeling it press forward and in.

Ankle angulation exercise. Even with the burliest slalom boot, you can get a little angle in the ankle. Think about making a series of long, slow turns just by inverting your foot inside your boot, feeling pressure on the inside ridge of your foot. Lift your inside ski off the snow when you do this, and concentrate on standing upright.

Ski Feel Drills

The performance skier is completely comfortable on his skis, as if they were part of his body. It takes experience to achieve this familiarity.

Side-camber turn. On a flat slope, center your

weight over your inside leg and lay the outside ski on its edge. Don't flex forward or push. Let the ski arc naturally. Skis will arc, some just barely. In any case, your turning radius will be immense.

Flat-ski wiggles. I saw Billy Kidd do this years ago at the international team races in Sun Valley. I was on the cat track below the roundhouse and watched with amazement as he pivoted thirty degrees from one side to the other with no edge whatsoever. I tried it, caught an edge, and went sailing off the cat track into the woods. Do this slowly on smooth, flat slopes. It takes a lot of touch; keep your feet close together.

Lead-change turn. This is a good way to get the feel for gliding turns. The turn is made the same way you would make an easy turn on in-line skates, by advancing one foot ahead of the other. Let your skis run down a smooth slope at a good clip. Push one foot ahead of the other by at least a half-boot length. You will see that you can generate a long-radius turn from nothing more than this shuffle. Think about how a lead change fits in when making normal high-speed turns on the groomed.

Loose-boots drill. This could just as easily come under balance, pressure, or edging drills. Simply undo your buckles, let your feet get nice and loose inside the boots, then make turns down the hill. It's not easy, but you learn to use subtly the little muscles of your feet.

Synchronized Drills

Synchronized skiing is one way to play at being a Blue Angel. It runs against the grain of lots of good skiers because it's organized. Still, it's great for improving your skiing; it makes you responsive to outside cues. In free skiing, you cue on terrain. In racing, you key on poles. In synchro skiing, you key on your partner's turning radius, speed, and movements. There are many variations. For these three exercises, use yourself and a partner. Once you've gotten good at it, try it in the bumps.

Figure 8s. In theory, this is easy; one person simply follows the other. The follower should concentrate on matching each aspect of his partner's turns: pole-plant timing, turn shape and radius, amount of vertical movement, stance, and hand position. This drill is good preparation for the next two.

The weave. This is a fairly simple beginning exer-

Left: The figure 8 is the simplest synchronized partner drill, especially if you and your partner agree on the width of your turning corridor before starting. Focus on the lead skier's arm swing and pole plant to maintain your rhythm.

Center: The weave is exciting because it involves repeated near-collisions. Develop a rhythm by concentrating on the lead skier's arm swing.

Right: The four-four-four is challenging and should be practiced on smooth terrain before attempted on rougher surfaces.

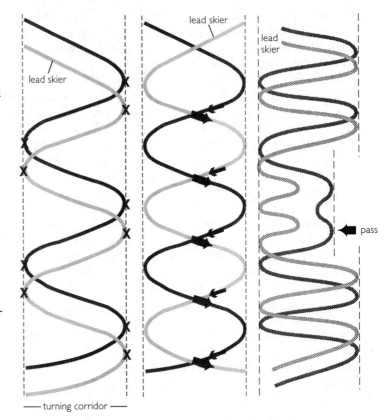

— turning corridor —

cise. Agree to use a fixed medium- or long-radius turn. Starting from the same point, head off in diverging traverses, then turn back in toward each other. On the first crossing, pass behind your partner; on the second, pass ahead of him. The passing point should also be the initiation–weight transfer point for both. Keep this up as long as you can. You must constantly gauge your speed, angle, and turning radius against your partner's to avoid a collision. This is the hazard—and the challenge.

The four-four-four. This is more difficult. You synchronize with the leader, who makes four medium turns, then pass in sync as you both do four short turns. Then you become the leader, moving smartly back into four medium turns. This can be repeated all the way down the hill. You don't follow the other skier's tracks, but you make the same-radius turn at the same time behind him, as if you were skiing eights. If someone were looking up the hill, you would be almost obscured by the leader as you made the first four turns. When the leader commences the short turns, you want to delay your first short turn so you can move alongside him. You then shorten up your radius, but not as much as the previous leader, so your faster speed will get you around him before you start the longer turns. About the second short turn, you are abreast and going in the same direction. Remember, you want to edge set and transfer your weight simultaneously. After passing during the four short turns, you enlarge the radius for the longer turns as your partner now gets in sync with your turns. Two helpful hints: Both skiers should count out loud at first; if your first turn is to the left, pass to the left.

Air Tips

This is one of the most enjoyable aspects of skiing. Even for advanced skiers, it takes practice to get comfortable in the air. Don't push it; start on little kickers and build up to the Scott Schmidt-class cliffs.

Straight shot. Take charge. Never feel like the terrain launched you. You should feel like you jumped it. This keeps your head and body going downhill and not coming back onto the tails of your skis with your arms doing the reverse backstroke. As you approach, flex the legs, then extend on the lip, pushing your hands down and forward. Retract your legs through your heels to keep the tips down. Spread your legs slightly and extend them just before touchdown to absorb the impact. Try not to break at the waist, but sink through with your rear end and land on two feet.

Bank shot. If you take a bank shot coming onto a jump—not straight on, but in a turn—you must keep your outside arm continuously moving toward the outside of the turn. This will keep you from doing a major hip check on touchdown. It also helps to extend your outside leg as much as possible to contact the snow early. This kind of jump-turn is dramatic, but predict how much air time you'll encounter. Don't forget that as long as the skis are on the ground, they are turning. In the air, direction of flight is a straight line tangent to the turning radius at the point you leave the ground. You should calculate how much angle your skis should have in relation to the direction of flight. The longer the air time, the narrower the skis' angle should be to the fall line.

To do a good hop turn, you must center your weight on your skis and rotate them enough that they won't slip downhill when you land. As Lloyd Scroggins does, finish each leap by sinking to prepare for the next one.

Crud Tips

Move your weight back onto your heels to allow the tips to plane, but that's about it. Even in the densest crud—deep, wet, heavy, cut-up snow—try to remain centered on the ski. Forget steering the skis in deep crud unless you have excellent touch. It's best to get up out of the snow and turn the skis in the air, pivoting with the feet. Set up with a couple of good accordion-type rising and sinking moves to get a feel for the density of the snow. You have to think "pop."

Garlands. This is an excellent way to get your body moving up and down. A garland is performed from a descending traverse and is a series of linked uphill turns along the traverse. You turn the skis uphill each time you sink down on them. When you extend, the tips tend to drop back on your line. Once you get a little rhythm going, turn the last extension into a turn down the hill.

Hop turns. Even in dense crud, you can find some "ramp" that will get the tips out. If you don't make it all the way around, no big deal—just do it again. Depending on the conditions, you may need two, three, or more hop-and-pivots to complete one turn. Move from one turn into another, using the natural flex of the ski for rebound. Prepare for this by making one turn on good terrain through the use of three or more hops and small, foot-steered pivots.

ELEVEN

Racing Basics

EXCELLENT FREE SKIERS often have trouble when they try racing. The reason is simple. Tactics—at what point you take specific actions—are critical to racers but a rare consideration among free skiers unless they're on seriously difficult terrain. Refining your line and timing takes thought and practice. That's why racing, regardless of format, is good for any skier who wants to improve. Technique, fairly constant among all skiers, is not enough; you have to develop tactical skills.

Racing is the best way to challenge yourself physically and develop those skills. It's one thing to ski all day; it is another to train on an equivalent number of race runs. Racing puts demands on your body that you rarely encounter otherwise. To hold a tight line when you are arcing a fast giant slalom turn on hard snow requires strong body angulation, dynamic moves, and an aggressive attitude.

For nonracers, what you learn while out on the racing hill will immediately affect your free skiing. Unless you belong to a U.S. Ski Association racing program, most races you encounter will be either slalom or giant slalom. As exciting as the downhill and Super G events are, they will be touched on only briefly here.

Slalom

Since the advent of the self-redressing pole or rapid gate in slalom, tactics and—to some extent—technique have changed in slalom racing. Some skiers have shied away from single-pole slalom racing because the prospect of skiing through a pole rather than around it is intimidating. The modern slalom skier looks like RoboCop, decked out in pads and armor. Some complain that rapid gates have destroyed the style and grace of slalom. Many slalom skiers do shin the pole, throw the skis sideways, stomp on the edge, and go straight at the next, all the time flailing to stay in balance and on the course. Nevertheless, the masters can be incredibly agile and graceful, such as Alberto Tomba, Marc Girardelli, Armin Bittner, Vreni Schneider, Petra Kronberger, and Tamara McKinney. They ski a rounder line, letting the ski do the work and getting more energy out of it.

Many who would try slalom are still wrestling with the idea of rapid gates. Not knowing quite what to do as they hurtle into a thicket of poles, they punch away with abandon. The skier who does not change his technique when skiing giant slalom will often change his short-turn technique dramatically in a rapid gate course. Remember that the object is not to knock over

Eva Twardokens of the U.S. Ski Team practices her slalom technique with stubbies. Because her upper body is facing downhill, she can make a great change of direction in a very short distance.

as many gates as you can, but to get down the course as fast as you can. The skis must go around the pole in a smooth, carving manner, so think more about your feet than your arms. The slalom skier also needs excellent balance, coordination, agility, and power.

Using baby gates or stubbies (knee-high rapid gate poles with padded tops) helps you learn to run gates without the distraction of poles flying around your upper body. At first, if you take a pole in the face too often, you will become stiff and defensive. Understand that the fastest route down the course is the one that moves your center of mass back and forth across the fall line as little as possible. This was even true with nonhinging gates, but because the skis and your center both had to be on the same side of the pole, it wasn't important. Your skis may turn around the pole, but if your center is inside its vertical plane, you will be faster than if your center were outside it.

PHASES OF THE TURN. Slalom technique and tactics depend on terrain and conditions. We will once more break up an ideal turn for analysis. Remember the four phases: preparation, initiation, controlling or steering, and finishing. They are just as valid in slalom racing, but a couple of refinements are also needed. Say the slalom racer has just arrived at a gate.

Edge set. Depending on the condition of the course, the racer will use a powerful inward movement of the ankles, knees, and hips. In rapid gates, the edge set comes later than in past years; the racer lets the skis run farther down the fall line before setting the edge. When done effectively, these become J-turns (or, in the extreme, Z-turns). If the course is rutted, steep, or your edges are not holding well, a rounder turn is needed. The important factors are positioning the distance of the ski from the pole and adjusting the turning radius for maximum carving of the outside ski. The hallmark of the elite slalom skier is a large change of direction over a short vertical distance. This requires quick reflexes and strong legs.

Foot push. From the edge set, the outside ski begins to carve through the turn. At the end of the carve, the skilled racer often pushes the carving ski forward a few inches, like a knife slicing cleanly through a tomato. Foot push reduces the angle at the knee and

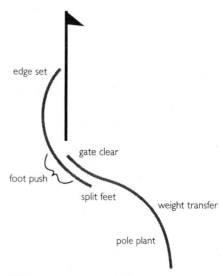

When practicing slalom turns, concentrate on each element individually before putting them all together.

shifts the weight back onto the tail of the ski, allowing for better edge hold through the last part of the turn. This move is not pressure redistribution onto the tail by sinking the hips. It happens so quickly in slalom that it is hard to see, and takes considerable strength and skill.

Gate clear. Knocking the slalom pole aside is called a gate clear. Ingemar Stenmark was the first to figure out how to do this properly. He was one of the few racers who won World Cup slaloms before and after the advent of rapid gates. Depending on distance from the gate, the pole can be taken out with the outside arm, inside arm, or occasionally across the body. The "body slam" is usually not a good idea, as the pole causes friction as it slaps into you. You also have a good chance of getting smacked in the face, or at least flinching. Remember, shin to win; face to place.

You will probably develop a preference in arm clearing. The best competitors are ambidextrous. From the inside, the arm is driven through the pole and forward, which brushes it to the side. This method helps eliminate overrotating. When doing an outside-arm clear, or reverse block, keep your shoulders level and isolate the movements of your arm from your upper body so as not to overrotate. This is very difficult because of

A Swedish Ski Team racer executes an outside arm clear. Using a short punch, he moves the gate without overrotating his upper body.

the tendency to twist the torso in the same direction when you bring your outside arm across your body, or to lean toward the pole with the upper body. Many coaches do not like teaching outside clears in rapid gates to younger skiers until they have developed strong fundamental skiing skills.

In an outside clear, the skier generates substantial forward force through the pole. If your hand is ready to hit the pole and you pop it forward just before you ski into the gate, you can overcome the pole's inertia and move it away from you faster than your body is moving. You can hit the pole with the back of your hand or forearm, but the best spot may be with your ski pole, right below your little finger. You should rotate your wrist inward so that the pole becomes nearly perpendicular to the slalom pole. With the narrow ski pole shaft, you can hit the slalom pole solidly and it slides off the shaft quickly.

You must hit the pole between mid-chest and shoulder level. If the hands are low or the skier is out of position, several problems arise: You may try to protect your face, affecting balance; you may flinch and sit back; or the pole may first hit your shin, bending the pole back into your face. If you take most of the pole contact at or below the shins, you generally are taking too straight a line. Shin level is the pole's stiffest point. The friction slows you down, or the pole may spin you around. Take a slightly rounder line and make higher initial contact with the pole, where there is less resistance.

Occasionally, the skis' sidewalls can break when running rapid gates, because the gate slams down on top of a ski that is highly stressed torsionally. Skiers often add protective neoprene or silicone strips to the top of their skis. Also, pads are essential over the knees and shins. A pole taken across the shins or, worse, the kneecap, can be very painful. Slalom helmets, bands, and forearm pads also are available, and some women use chest protectors. I've picked up teeth from the snow, left by people who weren't using a tooth guard.

Split feet. At the pole, the skis diverge and the inside one takes a higher line, which also brings the inside leg into an A-frame position under the skier.

This move allows the outside ski to run out carving through its natural turning radius and permits strong steering or pivoting of the uphill ski later in the turn as it becomes the outside ski. This takes strength and ability usually seen in mature racers.

Some skiers lock their feet too tightly together, which causes the inside ski, boot, and lower leg to block movement of the outside leg. A wider stance at the gate can put even more pressure on the inside ski. Keep the legs more independent vertically. By raising the knee of the inside leg, the outside one can articulate naturally as it finishes through the turn. With a vertically independent inside leg, the movement of the inside knee is pronounced and forceful, and it assists with the gate clear.

Weight transfer. The weight transfer is a positive step onto the new outside ski that follows naturally from the diverging movement of the feet through the gate. The move needs to be made with authority and commitment. In slalom, the transfer frequently will be made onto an uphill ski that has been rotated partially into the direction of the new turn. This gives a char-

Former Junior Alpine Racer of the Year Tim Curran performs a strong inside-arm gate clear, keeping his shoulders and arms level and angulating his hips.

Coming across the hill, he again uses his left arm (now on the outside) to clear the gate. With his center of mass well inside the pole, he travels the shortest and most direct route possible.

Curran shifts his weight onto his uphill ski but delays setting the edge so that he can better glide to the next turn. Note that his pole plant occurs midway between gates as he unwinds his lower body in the direction of the next turn.

Curran's powerful edge set arcs his skis at the crux of the turn. Although his stance is a little narrow, he moves through the gate with his inside knee advanced and feet slightly split.

acteristic wedge-turn look. When a quick change of direction is needed, the racer may not transfer the weight until after the knees cross over the skis. This means he turns on the inside ski. Although the initiation can be made with the skis slightly fanned or on the inside ski, clean, technical skiing is done best with the skis parallel and weight transferred solidly from one foot to the other.

Pole plant. At high levels of racing, the pole plant, when used at all, takes place not at the gate, but far-

Pressuring the skis evenly, he advances the downhill one with a forward-foot push. Although a bit over-rotated, he is stable, relaxed, ready, and focused on the next gate.

ther downhill, halfway between gates, to keep the flow going. The plant is very light; elite racers rely on better balance rather than a jammed pole plant. In the model turn, the pole plant is just a flicker at the wrist. Many racers also are tending toward slightly longer poles to keep the hands higher at the gate.

SLALOM DRILLS. There are many drills to teach slalom technique. If you have access to slalom poles and you have someone who can help set, reset, and pull the course when you're done, the following drills can refine your gate-running skills.

Sideslip course. Slalom skiers need to have good sensitivity in their feet and control of their edges. Set a corridor and sideslip through at varying speed, using both skis or just one for slipping, or sharp edging to a stop.

Side hill course. The side hill course is essentially a long flush, diagonal to the fall line, or the gates can be slightly offset. After setting a half-dozen or so in one direction, bring the course back across the fall line. When running on the side hill, accentuate the edge set on the downhill side while trying to get more glide on the uphill with a strong unweighting off the outside ski.

Pole jungle. Take twenty or so poles and set them randomly in a loose cluster. Skiers enter the cluster with no predetermined route. The object is to react quickly, choosing different lines and poles to go around. Set the jungle with hinged gates to avoid the bowling-pin syndrome.

Jump-turn course. Set a tight flush of ten to twenty poles. They should be no more than a half-ski length apart. Try to turn around each pole without knocking it down. Approach the space between the first two poles with a broad angle to the pole line. Ski slowly and allow the tails to just clear the upper pole. Change directions with a strong up movement and pivoting of the skis in the air. When the skis touch down, keep from skidding or slipping sideways. You should now be able to repeat the movement in the opposite direction between poles two and three. As you get better, you should be able to do this with steeper angles.

Rhythm course. Set a symmetrical series of turns, then a flush series, repeating this sequence down the

Set a rhythmic, tight, round course to develop good vertical movement and foot steering. Be patient when skiing this course; you should be able to carry just enough speed to travel smoothly from one turn to the next.

hill. Set an odd number of poles in each so that the skier exits each section in the same direction he entered. The purpose is to get used to rhythm changes and to figure out how to enter long turns from short ones and vice versa. Basically, you can take the last gate of the long-turn section straighter. The transition from short turns to long requires more direction on the last turn.

Obstacle courses. There are lots of combinations. Set two sets of poles in an X, then lay another pole across. The skier must lie on the back of the skis to pass under. Do the same with the horizontal pole lower to the ground, so that the skier has to jump. Set a loose couple of slalom poles, then come out of the fall line with a pole that the skier first turns underneath, but then has to skate and step up and around.

Lay poles zigzag on the ground. The skier first has to jump from one side to the other so that both skis touch the ground, then, without breaking rhythm, slightly change direction and again jump back and forth over the poles. Do this for about six pole lengths.

Arm-clear course. This drill teaches you to become ambidextrous in rapid gates. Set two stubbies even to each other and perpendicular to the fall line. Then set a full-length pole down the fall line, halfway between the stubbies above. Move down the hill, repeating with two more stubbies and a long pole until you run out of poles. You now have two symmetrical courses, each starting with a turn toward the long pole from whichever stubby you wish to begin. Change the arm clear you use on both sides.

Let's say you start with the stubby on the left looking down the hill. All turns around long poles will be to your left. You can do a complete run with only outside clears using your right arm. The next run starts with the stubby on the right. All turns on the long pole will be to the right, and your outside clear is with your left arm.

On your third and fourth runs, use inside clears only. This really simplifies learning arm clears, as you only work one side and method at a time.

Air traffic control course. Set three courses side by side. The coach at the bottom of the hill indicates which course the racer should switch to by waving the poles one way or the other. The racer must keep the courses in sight as well as key off of the coach.

Rut course. If the snow is soft, set a course with lots of turns, angling the poles toward the inside of the turns. Set it so that the skier can maintain momentum without having to hop turns. Run the course without resetting until you have deep, round ruts. Pull or reset once unsafe holes develop.

A rutted course requires different tactics. If you try to ski next to the pole in a deeply rutted course, it is likely your tails will slide off the bank and down into the rut. Any bobbles like this will slow you down considerably. Forget about clearing the poles and concentrate on riding the banks for maximum speed.

The most common errors in rut riding are leaning in so you can't shift the weight to a new downhill ski, and sitting back so that you get ejected from the course. To keep from leaning in, angulate sharply in the hips and aggressively drive your outside arm away from the center of the turn. Don't step or transfer your weight until your skis move back underneath your hips. Because your skis are moving much faster than your upper body, if your hips are behind your bindings as your skis come underneath you, they will squirt out faster than you can react. Without overloading the tips, ski ruts in a low, forward position, as if you were sprinting out of the chocks on a track.

long pole

stubby

inside clear
with right arm
or
outside clear
with left arm

inside clear
with left arm
or
outside clear
with right arm

The stubbies in an arm-clear course allow you to regroup and rebalance before attempting the next long pole. Concentrate on developing proper technique with one arm at a time.

If your technique is good, ride the rut with the outside ski while the inside leg is more nearly vertical underneath you and close to the inside pole. While your outside ski rockets around the bank, you actually define your line by the shorter arc of your inside ski.

Endurance course. Try setting super-long courses. Don't make them too technical or worry about speed, but complete every run. This is demanding and requires concentration. Such courses are particularly useful early in the season but after skiers have done more basic slalom drills.

Giant Slalom

Giant slalom became an official International Ski Federation (FIS) event in 1946. Previously, it was used to teach young racers technique they would use in downhill. In the early days, one-run GSs could last three minutes or more. Though considerably shorter, modern GS requires great technique and strength. It's won through precision, yet it gives you a wild ride.

Slalom looks like a forest of poles littering the hill. As soon as you make one turn, you usually jump into the next. In GS, you have to have patience, and your speed allows little margin for error. It has been called the most tactically and physically demanding of all alpine events.

Line is most critical in GS. Gates are staggered much farther across the hill, which means that as you approach one, the next leaves your peripheral vision. The forces acting on your body are so much greater than in slalom, or even fast recreational skiing, that it takes a lot of strength to resist them.

There is a much greater range of body positions, from a crouch with your rear end inches from the ground, to standing almost erect at turn initiation. Much of what was discussed in Chapter Nine can be applied to GS. There are some specific things about it, however. GS racing has evolved. There is now increased emphasis on carving throughout a turn, then moving directly into the next without a lateral step uphill. There was a time when it was important to make a big step onto the uphill ski, pushing off with the downhill one to step into a higher line. This was almost a requirement in the 1970s because of ski design. Racers needed the big step uphill to maintain

their line. As design and materials improved, manufacturers tuned skis' rigidity for optimum grip and
flex. Better vibration dampening has meant smoother,
more stable rides, which also allow racers to ski
rounder lines.

Though a big lateral step is still important when you
lose your edge or are too low, a premature step off the
downhill ski releases the pressure on the edge and all
the potential spring is lost. You want to link carved
turns and flow from one into the next. Exactly when to
apply pressure depends on the situation. If you are
scrambling, begin to drop onto the ski immediately. If
you remain extended a little longer, the ski will drift
into the next turn and you can redirect it with a little
foot steering.

For most racers, the most difficult factor in GS is
holding the last part of the turn, when forces are greatest. It is crucial to know when and where to initiate the
turn. Former U.S. Ski Team coach Harald Schoenhaar
developed a timing aid based on the rise line and rule
of thirds. In GS, you initiate your turn as you intersect
the rise line—the imaginary line from the turning pole
directly uphill along the fall line. As you go around the
turning pole, your skis should be pointed two-thirds of
the distance from the next turning pole to the near

*Swedish team member Lars
Eriksson keeps his hips low
at the first gate and then
rises between turns, bringing hips and hands forward.
He edges his skis by leaning
his upper body toward the
inside of the turn and exits
ready for the next turn.*

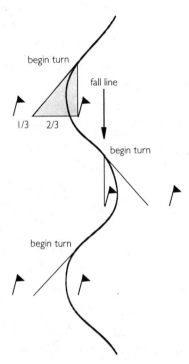

When running gates, concentrate on turn timing and approach angle. Initiate each turn directly above the turning pole and point your skis at a spot two-thirds of the way from the inside pole to the outside one. In slalom, where the turn radius is shorter, point your skis toward a spot one-third the distance between the two poles.

pole of the outside gate. Obviously, much depends on terrain, speed, and conditions. Although this may seem difficult to calculate at full tilt, with a little practice, you can develop a much clearer sense of position when you are on course.

Similarly, many coaches teach "coming underneath the pole." Look at the pole from above, with twelve o'clock pointing directly down the fall line. When you pass the turning pole, the angle of your skis to the pole should be tangent to the eleven o'clock position on the pole in a right turn and at one o'clock turning left. In other words, finish one turn as much as possible before you go by the pole.

Racing is a game of risk. The winner is the one who takes the most chances yet maintains control. If we're skiing equally fast but your turning radius is consistently three inches shorter on a fifty-gate course than mine, at the finish I may have skied fifteen feet farther than you. Do that over two runs, and I'll be a half-second or so off your time. So how tight a line can you shave and still keep it together? You have to experiment. When you first start racing, you should ski as well as you can, but your top goal is to finish. Later, you can pull out the stops. As you gain experience, you can run courses a little straighter to cut the distance. The trade-off is that you must change the direction of your skis even faster. To hold the edge, you'll need much stronger legs and better technique.

Most skiers don't realize how quickly they can change direction, even on long GS skis, and still hold a clean edge. Try this: Get out your GS skis and find a hill with good pitch and some bumps. Ski diagonally across at first, with a shallow angle to keep your speed down. Absorb the bumps in your legs. At the end of your traverse, pick a bump off of which you can pop. With a lot of upper-body anticipation, your skis will come around almost 180 degrees. Land on the edge of your downhill ski and traverse in the other direction with little or no skidding. Do airplane turns and land with such balance that your edge sets and carves cleanly. This takes a lot of sensitivity and touch. As you improve, you should be able to transfer this to a smoother hill where, instead of launching yourself, you can get the same radical change of direction with your skis on the snow—again, with no sliding or skidding. Clean turns require strong unweighting to allow the skis to pivot; big crossovers to get the ski up on edge; a good, countered, balanced position on the outside ski; and sinking in the hips to absorb the shock of the skis biting into the snow. If you can transfer this skill to the racecourse, you will be able to ski shorter, thus faster, lines. Just don't overdo it, either as an exercise or on a racecourse. That's dancing with the devil.

GS DRILLS. Most of these are timing and tactic exercises. Helper poles or markers indicate where to initiate a turn or where the coach wants the skier to go. At the Timberline Race Camps on Mount Hood, colorful feather dusters are used.

Helper poles. These usually are set on the rise line and from four to nine feet above the pole. They are placed so that if the skier turns at one, his skis will be fully turned in the new direction as he passes the turning pole. If you use a helper pole, angle it inward so the skier does not have to duck or counter it to go around. Markers may also be set below the turning pole; stay above it to keep a close high line just below the pole.

Sink poles. Set a pole below the turning pole and angle it uphill so that its tip just touches the turning pole about four feet off the snow. The skier must pass through this little triangle. To do so, he must crouch very low, coinciding with the point where he should have maximum pressure on his skis. Don't bend forward at the waist to duck under; this is ineffective and defeats the purpose of the drill.

Corridors. Corridors require work to construct and concentration from the skier. They can seem intimidating, yet many skiers who try them enjoy the challenge. The skill of the skiers should be considered when selecting the pitch of the hill and turning radius of the corridor. Better skiers can manage corridors on fairly fast hills and just before steeps. A good corridor can use as many as twenty-four to thirty poles in addition to the standard GS gate, which is still called for. The setter visualizes the proper line and makes a passageway with bamboo poles. The corridor should be like a funnel—wide at the mouth and then tapered. The skier will ski around the turn, coming into the traverse through the corridor. Corridors should be taken slowly at first, preferably in a wedge, to determine where the line should be. Use hinged gates on the downhill side so if the skier's line is too low, he won't hook tips. The last pair of poles of the traverse can be angled downhill so the skier knows that he must dive down the hill with his upper body. If he stands too erect and does not commit down the hill, the angled uphill pole will serve as an uncomfortable reminder.

Downhill and Super G

Unfortunately, getting experience in downhill is very difficult for many U.S. skiers. Frequently, the only training comes a day or two before a race. Many areas don't want the liability and are loath to close runs to the public. Good training courses require preparation, maintenance, and policing.

Despite these difficulties, speed events can be the most fun you can have short of flying supersonic aircraft. GS is fast but you still feel that you must put on the brakes to maintain your line. In downhill, you get the rare thrill of letting the skis run for all they are worth. Where downhill training can be found, it is frequently limited to section or element training. Super G is easier to set and prepare, and can teach good turning techniques at speed.

GLIDING. Some people think that the best downhillers have the straightest line and the flattest skis for maximum speed. This may apply on the flats and in straight schusses, but those are a very small part of most downhills. If you are going too fast and straight into a turn, the skis invariably are thrown sideways and there is a delay before the edge engages again. With each little skip, momentum is lost.

The ski is on one edge or the other 95% of the time. Gliding is the ability to keep the momentum going from one turn to the next, carrying speed and linking turns from one to the next. To maintain proper contact with the snow, the skier must stay loose in both the hips and the ankles.

TURNING. When you enter a new turn at speed, it's essential that your torso move into it first. It doesn't matter so much which foot you're coming off, but your upper body must come forward and across the skis. If you're back or neutral, you'll move into the turn too slowly. As the body crosses the skis, transfer your weight. To get pressure on the tip and to the outside ski, bend your ankle at the beginning of the turn.

Because your skis will go in the direction of your upper body, anticipate coming into the turn. The skis will jet out if you don't anticipate well. If the tip of the inside ski goes down as it comes around, you have made a good crossover with your head ahead of your feet. As soon as you feel pressure on the outside ski, you have to resist rotation of your upper body. Particularly at speed, the ski is going to break loose and skid as soon as you overrotate.

The movement down on the ski needs to be slowed so that steady pressure is maintained throughout the turn. Also, keep a long outside leg, to use the skeletal structure rather than leg strength, as when holding a bent knee, for support.

TRAVERSING. This is important for downhillers because the distance between turns is so long. Some skiers make a pretty turn, but the traverse gets "soft" as they turn square to the tips and reduce pressure on the edge, trying to ride flatter skis. Again, speed is lost.

Practice long traverses across the hill at speed and at increasingly steeper angles. Find the balance point of the ski and the optimum position with which to hold a good edge and maintain suppleness over the snow. This can be done on moguled as well as groomed slopes, though things can get hairy if you lose it in the bumps.

TUCK TURNS. Work into high-speed turns by practicing tuck turns on groomed slopes. When the surface is more rippled, speeds seem higher. To absorb rougher terrain, stand taller to free the legs. All the elements in a high-speed tuck turn are the same as in any turn. You may be in a tuck, but your upper body still determines the direction of travel. Flatten the ski out, and as the tips begin to come around, cross over the skis with your upper body, putting forward pressure on the tips.

As the skis come out of the fall line, you can keep the body blocked up following the tips around, which puts you on your inside foot and unable to hold the outside edge. Don't stand on two feet to make the skis go faster and lessen the pressure on the outside ski. Stand on the outside ski.

AIR TIME. The good downhill or Super G skier is comfortable in the air. Working your way from the one-meter board to a high-dive tower takes practice and patience; so do progressively longer flights on skis. There are three ways to deal with terrain that can launch you.

The press. When you press from a nearly erect position, move up and forward slightly with your hips and hands. Pull your feet up and move your hands forward. This moves your center of mass down toward the terrain. Many times the press is attempted by pushing the hands forward but the rear end stays back, which causes the tips to get uncomfortably light. To avoid this, pull your heels and the tails of your skis up while staying aerodynamic. A two-footed touchdown provides the best control.

The prejump. These are fun. If you come to a roll and jump into the air before the lip, you will float over the crest and land on the downhill side without being launched. To have a good prejump on snow means you should have a good jump on dry land. To prejump from a tuck, your body should extend fully and smoothly, then you pull both legs up.

A good way to develop a strong prejump is to take slalom poles and lay them in the snow before the crest so that you have to clear them. Practice prejumps while free skiing.

The pop. Sometimes in a downhill you may want to jump. It's not always faster to stay on the ground. As long as you stay aerodynamic, you've eliminated friction of the ski on the snow. In the case of a double bump, you may be faster popping off the first one and floating over the second rather than trying to press or prejump both. The pop is more than just riding over rolls; it involves a quick straightening of the legs right on the crest. You don't have to have double rolls, but you should have a good downhill outrun to practice. Jumping is also good for spatial awareness and balance.

TWELVE

Tech Talk: Your Gear

SKIERS HAVE CONTROL over their physical condition, technique, attitude, and equipment. Let's look at modern equipment and how to maximize its use.

There are lots of buying guides that explain skis and boots, and how to tune, repair, and adjust. Most of the information is worthwhile, but equipment is changing so fast that it is hard to stay up with it. The following combines advice on how to keep your equipment in good condition plus background information. Some of it may dispute commonly held beliefs. Even in the high-technology world of skiing equipment, there is as much art as science.

Skis

Every year, new skis with bright graphics come on the market, and every year, new buzzwords arise for the latest breakthroughs in technology. Reality is often lost in the marketing hype. From one brand to another, it's simply a matter of personal preference. The level of technology is high and the market is extremely competitive, so for specific performance, there really are no bad skis on the racks anymore. Manufacturers use different materials, construction, and geometry, but they all are looking for durability, stability, agility,

165

and speed. What is perhaps more amazing is how this can be achieved in so many different ways.

Skis have evolved over the last thirty years from wood laminates with screw-on metal edges to composite marvels of wood, metal, fiberglass, Kevlar, carbon, ceramic, foam, and viscoelastic rubbers. Many performance characteristics have changed. Unfortunately, some of the things that were true about skis then are still assumed about skis today.

FLEXIBILITY. Skis must have camber and some rigidity to evenly distribute the weight of the skier. They must be supple enough to bend into an arc when they are weighted in a turn and have enough rigidity to snap back to their original shape in the transition phase. Skis also must resist twisting. Too much, and the ski will bounce out of its arc; too little, and the ski will roll off its edge. Performance skis, particularly those for slalom, need a fair amount of torsional rigidity. Years ago, manufacturers had difficulty building this in without also making the ski longitudinally quite stiff. Consequently, good skiers all needed stiff skis. Then they would dive onto the tips to make the ski bend and try to do a kip-up off the tails to keep up with the ski as it vaulted out of the turn.

Today, manufacturers better isolate these two variables, making the skis torsionally stiff, yet supple in their length. This means a smoother ride in bumps and better contact with the snow. It also makes the skis much faster, since too-stiff ones tend to skid and scrub off speed. Skis also can now be made with variable torsional rigidity. The tips and tails are just a little softer so they don't hook or hang up, but the skis have great edge-hold underfoot.

CORES. Foam cores were introduced not long ago. They have some great properties, including lightness, but the first foam cores weren't very durable. Improved chemistry, new kinds of foam, torsion box construction, vibration absorption, and reinforcing materials now make foam core skis every bit as durable and smooth as wood core skis. Some skiers still think you can tell the difference by tapping the tails on the ground and listening to the pitch. With the variety of composite cores, this has become another old wives' tale. True, almost every downhill ski is now made with a simple wood-fiberglass-metal laminate, but good recreational cruisers, slaloms, and GS skis can be found in either foam or wood.

The use of Kevlar, graphite, and ceramic has become common, and more new materials are on the horizon. Kevlar is five times stronger than steel, is twice as stiff as fiberglass, and has high vibration-damping characteristics. Graphite and ceramic also provide stiffness and vibration damping. These materials are all expensive.

One point of debate has been that some manufacturers highly tout these materials but only include token amounts in their skis. On the other hand, it may not take much to achieve the desired effect.

GEOMETRIES. These have gained a lot of attention recently. With the advent of the hinged gate for slalom, racers wanted skis that could make a fast direction change but resist coming back across the hill at the end of the turn (the J-turn).

The Atomic HV-3 slalom was one of the first of these skis. It had a narrow tip, wide tail, and a side cut farther forward than previous skis. It had a narrow taper angle, formed by running imaginary lines along the lengths of the ski tangent to the tip and tail. Classic slalom skis such as the Rossignol 4S or Blizzard V20 Thermo had a wide taper angle with a wide shovel and narrow tail.

It's not quite so simple anymore. Rapid-gate skis are available in narrow or wide taper angles. Turn shapes are derived with a more complex mix of geometries and camber and flex patterns.

VIBRATION. Vibration dampening has also been much discussed recently. Manufacturers use a variety of internal and external systems to achieve this, such as the metal plates seen on Rossignols and Blizzards and the "dash-pot" devices on Dynastar and Spalding skis a couple of years ago. The Derbyflex plate, which mounts under the binding, is fairly popular among GS, Super G, and downhill skiers. Internally, cracked edges, the use of Kevlar, carbon, and ceramic, and constrained viscoelastic rubber sheets also reduce vibration.

Despite advertising claims, vibration dampening is still as much an art as a science. Laboratory measurements can show how various materials and constructions affect vibration at different frequencies, but correlations with skiers' impressions on snow have been elusive. About all that can be said definitively is that some dampening gives the ski a feeling of stability, yet too much makes it feel dead. Some systems work better than others at dampening some vibrations but may have little effect at other frequencies. Manufacturers have tended to concentrate on reducing vibrations at lower frequencies, but again, each has its own ideas.

SELECTION. It's easy to see how some of the old verities about ski design have become clouded. Some trends are clear, but be wary of pat assumptions when selecting skis. Slalom skis, the most popular high-performance selection, now have more narrow waists, are lighter than before, and are more supple in turns, allowing them to sneak and snake when the situation demands. They will provide a very solid bite, but you can get off the edge quickly. In GS skis, dampeners that isolate the foot are more prevalent. It may become more common for skiers to raise the foot off the ski a bit. GS skis run a poor second in sales, but as machine grooming and hill contouring increase, they may find more favor among performance skiers. Skis classified as "extreme" are in hot demand. They have GS characteristics but are a little softer torsionally and longitudinally. They are designed for all terrain and conditions. They are not deflected by ice balls, have good edge grip, and float in deep snow.

Of particular importance to today's skiers is maintenance. Because manufacturers have promoted their products as ready to go right out of the box, the public figures skis need less upkeep. Actually, for modern skis to perform at the level for which they were designed, they require much more maintenance, and manufacturers should provide more information on proper care.

Just remember that there is no best ski. The industry is sophisticated, and shop personnel can recommend models that fit your personality and skiing profile. It is much more difficult, however, for salespeople to know every detail of construction and how they affect performance for each ski on the rack. The best training for them is to try different models so they have a feel for each. When shopping for skis, don't arm yourself with one or two ideas about how skis are made and then play "stump the salesperson." Ask salespeople about their impressions of a ski and, when possible, to demonstrate different skis under a variety of conditions.

BASES. Years ago, all ski bases were made of extruded liquid polyethylene. All but the cheapest skis are now being manufactured with sintered bases. Sintering involves compressing polyethylene powder until it fuses into a disk about four inches wide. The disk is then skived to produce base material in continuous lengths. These bases are much harder and resistant to abrasion, yet are low in density and so are more permeable to wax than extruded bases.

How can a material be harder yet less dense? As the polyethylene fuses, it forms crystals that then form irregularly shaped grains. The crystals are extremely stable and strong, and the loose packing of the grains provides the low density. Extruded bases have a much less determinate structure and lack the porosity of sintered bases. A sintered base will absorb five times more wax than an extruded one.

P-tex, which has become the generic name for base material, is actually a trademark of Montana Sport. The Montana Sport company controls about 65% of the market for polyethylene bases. There is some confusion in stores because manufacturers rate the bases differently. There are at least ten grades of P-tex, from low molecular-weight extruded bases to extremely high molecular-weight sintered bases. These numbers are familiar as P-tex 2,000, 4,000, and 6,000, and Electra 2,000, 4,000, and 6,000. Another company, ISO, uses Type 7, Type 8, and Type 9 ratings. For the consumer, the distinction is largely irrelevant, as a ski maker will often use materials from all base manufacturers.

However, many skiers believe that the higher the rating number, the better the base. This is not entirely accurate. P-tex 2,000 has a molecular weight of 3.5 million; P-tex 6,000 has a weight of six million; but P-tex 4,000 has a weight of eight million. As the molecular weight goes up, the bases become more resistant to abrasion. You can make a slight indentation with a fingernail on a P-tex 2,000 base, but you can't on a P-tex 4,000. On the flip side, P-tex 2,000 may glide better at very low temperatures than the low-density 4,000. Some World Cup racers may have used high-density extruded bases in extremely cold weather. Composite bases of different sinter grades are designed to operate efficiently in a range of temperatures.

In 1984, Bill Johnson made the black base on his Atomics famous. A 10% to 15% mixture of graphite was added to P-tex to make the black or Electra base. The graphite makes the base conduct heat and electricity. Heat from friction is dissipated quickly, which helps reduce the water film under the ski, increasing glide. Also, static electricity is discharged, helping eliminate grime that can slow the ski down. The graphite increases density, however, making these bases less wax-absorbent. Still, since a graphite base is more irregular than a clear one, less structure is needed for good gliding.

Believe it or not, these bases once were unpopular with manufacturers because their logos could not be screened onto the bottoms. That was until World Cup racing results brought graphite to the forefront.

Plastics technology is ever on the move and new bases are being tested. In very limited production is a Teflon-Electra base of 70% Teflon and 30% graphite, which costs more than $60 for one pair of skis and may only be waxed with fluorocarbon compounds. Clear bases with Electra characteristics are on the horizon, as are bases that change color with temperature, potentially making waxing a snap.

Few skiers, elite racers excepted, select skis according to the base. Ninety percent of a ski's gliding and turning characteristics depend on tuning.

Tuning

After a skier finds the sweet spot on a ski, he can forget all about composition and construction and focus on maintenance. Don't kid yourself that a coat of wax every few weeks is all you need. The pilot is only as good as his ride.

INSPECTION. Modern skis are precisely made. Most manufacturers say skis are ready to go right out of the box, but since some of the larger firms can produce

2,000 pairs or more per day, there are occasional discrepancies. By the time you get them on snow, perhaps eight or nine months later, some aberrations may have set in, such as slight warping. These may be completely out of the hands of manufacturers, but don't assume all skis are ready to go out of the box. If you find discrepancies, you can easily get them reground.

Ask a qualified technician to show you how to properly inspect your skis if you don't know. Don't look foolish by trying to check quality control in a shop without knowing what to look for, and don't flex a ski by pressing on the base! Once you've found the model, type, and flex you like, quickly do these checks: Look for an even base pattern without dull or unpatterned spots. Hold a ski up to the light and use a true bar. Press the skis together and see how smoothly they mate. A tiny bit of double camber in the forebody is normal; triple camber isn't. Check for lateral misalignment by sighting down the skis from the tips. These are basically all the tests you need to know.

THE GRIND. Even after inspection at the store, you can assure that your new skis are flat with a shop stone grinding. If your skis are not new, have them ground when they show wear. If you ski across parking lots rather than powder, this will be pretty frequent. Check periodically for wear or unevenness with a true bar. If your skis are in good shape to begin with, they may need only five passes on the stone. Done a few times each season, you can get away with a $15 grinding as opposed to $40 worth of major work done once.

What's the difference between a stone grinder and a belt sander? The stone cuts base and edge material, whereas the sander "tears" the polyethylene, which

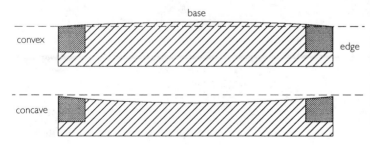

Check your skis' bases regularly. A convex base could be the result of a poor flat filing; a concave base could be a factory defect. Either problem can be corrected by having the bases stone-ground.

leaves a lot of tiny hairy fibers. The belt removes more base material than edge, so the ski becomes railed. After sanding, the edges must be filed down, then the bases scraped and polished with Fibertex. Lacking Fibertex, the more abrasive Scotch Brite pad is used to remove the friction-producing hairs.

One caution: The quality of stone grinding depends on the skill of the technician. Ground bases may not be perfectly flat if the technician does not dress the stone after every twenty or thirty pairs of skis. This does not take much time or effort, but it does wear down the stones, which cost money. Entire edges have been case-hardened from an improper stone grinding.

Stone grinding ensures a flat running base with structure—small grooves or rills running linearly or diagonally in a crosshatched manner. The rills provide channels for water. This reduces suction and increases gliding speed in warm snow. The more free water in the snow, the coarser the structure should be. In cold snow, where the crystals have sharp points, the structure allows air to flow under the ski, reducing friction. Linear rills are usual, as they work best at lower speeds and may increase stability. Diagonal crosshatched rills allow water to channel off more quickly by directing it to the edges. They are used primarily on speed, downhill, or super G skis. When a crosshatched structure is ingrained, the stone must

The stone grinder is a skier's best friend for getting skis into performance condition. Technicians like Brent Amsbury of World Cup Ski Tuning can restore the factory finish on a worn ski.

be turned very slowly so as not to damage the base.

If the structure starts to fade and you are low on funds, a riller bar (a piece of metal with fine ridges cut into it) can impress a new structure into the base. You will usually find fine and coarse groove frequencies on a riller bar. By asking your shop only to grind the bases, you should be able to save a little money. When you take your skis home, you get to do the beveling, edge polishing, and waxing.

HOME TUNING. Since you've been skiing for a while, you've collected some tools for a wax kit. There are several manuals and at least one videotape on the fine points of tuning and waxing. This discussion will concentrate on current essentials.

You should first know how to flat-file a ski. The idea is to keep the base flat by removing equal amounts of edge and base. The problem is that with sintered bases, only a new file will remove much base material. Besides being hard, sintered bases are elastic, so if the edge is beveled or the file unbowed, the file won't touch the edges. If it is bowed to contact the edge, you have little control over your bevel angle.

Consider beveling your edges, one at a time. Ensure your work is accurate with a true bar. When your base begins to show wear, get the skis stone-ground to ensure flatness and a refurbished structure.

THE BEVEL. New skis have a consistent edge angle

A true bar is an indispensable tool for the performance skier. While holding the bar against a ski's base, look for gaps between the two surfaces. When gaps appear, it's time to have the ski stone-ground.

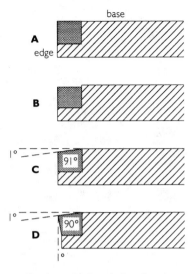

The bevel of a ski's edges greatly influences its performance. **(A)** A newly ground base will be flat and have ninety-degree edges. **(B)** Recessed edges reduce friction, but require special attention during stone grinding. **(C)** Beveling only the base edges causes skis to turn easily, but grip poorly on hard snow. **(D)** Beveling one degree off both the base and the side edges will maintain a ninety-degree angle. This edge will help skis turn smoothly and hold well on hard snow.

from end to end. The edges at tip and tail should be rounded to ensure smooth transitions from turn to turn. Start by rounding them conservatively and increase the roundness if the skis hang up in turns. If the tail protector is too square, you can round those angles to reduce drag and let the tail release cleanly.

Edges are beveled to allow the ski to roll up on edge a little more smoothly, like the hull chine of a boat. This also lets the skier extend his legs away from his center of mass a little more. Base-edge bevels are normally cut at one to three degrees. Skiers who make short turns use less bevel, from zero to one degree; skiers who prefer GS turns like one to one and a half degrees; and downhillers will use one to two and a half degrees. Ballet skiers may use four or more degrees to ensure edges don't catch during spins. Some may prefer a varied bevel along the length, decreasing under the foot, but this makes edge prep much more complicated, and few skiers can notice much difference.

The bevel on the base edge enhances turnability and glide. The side-edge bevel determines hold on the snow. If you bevel the base edge down one degree and the side edge is still perpendicular to the base, you will have a ninety-one-degree edge, which is "soft." This makes for easy turning with little hooking, and will work just fine in soft snow. For better grip, you will want to bevel the side edge back to keep the ninety-degree angle. Less than ninety degrees, and your edges will be quite sharp, grippy, maybe even hooky, and susceptible to damage if you hit a rock. Still, this is common for extreme ice.

When you bevel an edge, use a small, clean six- or eight-inch file. The smaller files work smoothly; larger files remove too much edge. Use a beveling tool. Some manuals show you how to use several wraps of tape around a file to get a bevel. If you're going to spend as much as $600 on skis, why would you not invest $10 to $50 on a beveling tool and eliminate the guesswork? The best device for a good base-edge bevel is a tapered sleeve, which is cheap and comes in an assortment of angles. You fit a six- or eight-inch file into one and lay it across the base. The file touches only the ski edge, and at the desired angle. Never file back into the base more than a quarter-inch.

For the side-edge bevel, there are a number of other tools. They all have a flange that lies flat on the base and supports the file against the edge. With most, you can dial in the angle you want. One of the best is the simplest. It is an L-shaped piece of aluminum and comes in premolded angles. There is a channel in the middle to allow filings to fall through so they don't get embedded in the file. Again, these are fairly inexpensive.

Machining or filing metal leaves burrs on the tapered edge. Remove these with 320 grit silicon carbide paper or a sharpening stone. Carborundum stones are popular; diamond stones are harder but more expensive. Rubber stones are handy and come in hard, medium, or soft grades. The soft one will conform completely to the edge and remove small burrs quickly while polishing.

WAXING. This not only allows skis to run faster but makes for easier turning and protects the base. Waxing can be as technical as you like. Consider a race technician who has to deal with snow temperature, air temperature, shape of snow crystals, free water in the snow, humidity, course length, weather patterns, shaded sections of the course, and the relative lengths of steeps and flats and where they are located. It takes experience to deal competently with all these variables.

Fortunately, it's easy to achieve good glide with regular, simple applications. Just follow the directions of the wax manufacturers. Polyethylene is somewhat unstable. When your bases are exposed to air and ultraviolet light, they oxidize, so keep your skis waxed and do not leave them in a rack with their bases up. The gray-white powder on the bases is a sign of neglect. New skis need a good coat of wax, and you should wax every time you ski. With new skis, hot wax them with an iron, then leave them in a warm place for a few days for maximum absorption. Scrape the skis, then wax again before you use them the first time.

Before waxing skis, clean the bases. There are a number of cleaners on the market, but it is more effective to clean by hot waxing, then warm scraping. Iron soft wax onto the base. Before it can cool, carefully remove it all with a plastic scraper. This may have to

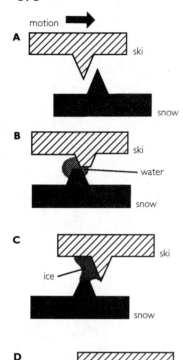

Waxing improves a ski's glide. (A) Microscopic irregularities exist in the ski's base. (B) As the ski passes over the snow, these irregularities collide with snow crystals, causing friction that melts snow. (C) Some of this free water refreezes, binding the snow to the base material and increasing the ski's sliding resistance. (D) When the ice bonds to a wax layer, however, the wax particles shear away easily, reducing resistance.

be done several times if your bases are really dirty.

There are many good waxes on the market, including Toko, Swix, and Briko. When you find a brand that works for you, stick with it. Keep a log of the conditions, the waxes you used, and how they felt. It won't take long to develop a system. Also, carry a good snow thermometer in your wax kit. Waxes use paraffin and hydrocarbon additives to create a barrier against water and reduce friction. A total of three or four waxes should cover the spectrum of temperatures and snow conditions. You usually won't need to mix more than two waxes for any situation. Hard waxes are for colder temperatures and softer ones for warmer.

If the snow is extremely abrasive, a hard wax will reduce penetration of the sharp crystals. A soft wax will work well if there is a lot of free water in the snow. Graphite would help in extreme cold or dirty snow. Black or Electra bases should be waxed regularly with special graphite wax. Over time, the graphite in the base erodes. To keep the bases in their original condition, this wax reimpregnates the base with graphite particles.

Fluorocarbon waxes, initially used for cross-country racing, are also available. Cera-F, a pure fluorocarbon, comes in a powder and is rubbed on. There are now bar fluorocarbon waxes that are also rubbed on. Fluorocarbon waxes are used in high humidity or warm snow. They are extremely fast because water on this surface has a low surface tension, like beads on a newly waxed car. For this excitement, you can pay $30 for one wax job. For a quick fix in warm weather, use liquid silicone in spray cans or wipe-on pads. Be sure to thoroughly clean your bases before rewaxing.

Sintered bases can absorb only a small amount of wax, so don't slop it on. The most important factor in wax absorption is the temperature of your iron. When the bases are heated, the amorphous areas expand and wax can penetrate, but don't overheat the core. This can weaken the resins holding it together. Swix recommends 212 to 248 degrees Fahrenheit for hydrocarbon waxes. If wax smokes or boils, it is too hot. Fluorocarbon waxes, in paste, powder, or bar form, should be applied according to manufacturer's recommendations.

Whenever you wax your skis, let them cool before scraping, preferably overnight. After scraping with a sharp plastic scraper, use a nylon brush down the length to bring out the texture of the structure. Polish with Fibertex or a Scotch Brite pad.

REPAIRS. Since skiing is done on the side of a mountain, sooner or later you're going to run over a nice, big rock. Previously, repairs could be made by letting a P-tex candle drip into the gouge. The material invariably was contaminated with carbon residue from the flame, so the bonding to waxed sintered bases was poor. If you ski a lot and want to keep your gear in good repair, buy an extrusion repair pistol, available for less than $150. Faced with the futility and frustration of candles and the cost of shop repairs, this is a pretty good deal, and pistols are easy to use. Similar to a glue gun, they melt high-grade polyethylene sticks and force them through a small nozzle into the gouge. The heat and pressure allow much better bonding. To assure this, you can undercut the gouge with an X-Acto knife. The sticks come in clear, black, and fluorescent colors, and in hardness for P-tex 2,000 and harder bases. Excess material is removed with a surform and file. Kits are available at your specialty shop.

Repairs can get a little more complicated if a gouge crosses a base groove. You can try a sharpened screwdriver to regroove your ski, but it's better to let a shop

An extrusion repair pistol can save you many trips to the ski shop and makes the P-Tex candle a thing of the past.

do this with a specialty tool. What about gouges next to an edge? Dripped candle P-tex won't hold against an edge. Extruded repairs done carefully with a warm ski will hold for a while. If the gouge is small, mix some epoxy resin and fill the hole. You won't notice any difference in your glide. If the gouge is big or down to the core, have a shop splice a new piece into the base.

When an edge hits a rock, the pressure creates enough momentary heat to case-harden it. Files are not hard enough to level most of these dings; a diamond stone is usually required. Minor tip and top sheet delaminations are still common. Carefully expand the delamination with a couple of screwdrivers. Let the damaged area dry thoroughly, pack the separation with epoxy, then, using metal scrapers on each side to distribute pressure, apply C-clamps. Remove any excess with a file.

If you take a serious header, always check your skis for bending. A minor bend may not be noticeable immediately, but when you resume skiing, turns on that ski may be skittery. To check for bending, press the skis together. Do they diverge anywhere below the normal tip-bend contact point? Obviously, a big bend ruins a ski. If it's not too great, have a shop warm the ski with lamps, then place it in a bending tool. This usually will bring the ski back close to its original shape. Many repair technicians prefer to have you do the rebending so that you don't accuse them in case the ski goes *blamo!* Although weakened, these skis will normally work just fine.

Boots

Good skiers can adapt their technique to almost any ski, but boots provide the link. They must transmit strong forces as well as small ones, and keep your feet comfortable and warm. They also must be affordable. In light of this, the choice of boots is amazing.

Economics requires manufacturers to build molds based on the average foot. Like the unicorn, the average foot is exceedingly rare. Almost 90% of the world's ski boots are made in a small region of Italy. Regardless of the integral high technology in modern manufacturing, many boots begin from wooden molds handcrafted by artisans. Because the dimensions of a foot don't change proportionately as the length changes, adjustments have to be made for different boot sizes, and one mold can cost $50,000.

SELECTION. Fit is the most important quality. Never mind the bells, whistles, or price. Fitting should be straightforward. Your toes should just touch the end of the boot, but they shouldn't be curled. You should not have any heel lift when you press forward, and your feet shouldn't go to sleep if you wear them for a while. If there is any question, pull out the liner and place your foot in the shell. Place your toes flush against the end and flex in the ankles. You should have one or two fingers worth of room behind your heel, no more. Wear the boots, flexing them as much as possible. If your shop has a Ski Legs device, lock your boots into it and wiggle around to simulate the flexing movements of skiing.

When choosing a boot, think about your biomechanics. A skier with long legs can generate a lot of torque. This skier needs a boot with a taller cuff but not as much forward stiffness. Because his leg will go through a greater range of motion, too much stiffness will put too much pressure on the tips abruptly, making control difficult. The skier with stubby legs needs a boot with a lower cuff and a little more stiffness. Because his leg travels less distance, he needs more response from the boot.

Proper boot flex allows you to keep your hips over your feet. If the boots are too stiff, you will have to flex in the waist to absorb bumps, so your hips get caught behind. This skier often seems to be squatting. Too much forward stiffness in a boot also can make you overpower your tips, making the skis hook.

Also, consider the kind of skiing you are doing. If you ski primarily bumps or all you do is big, round turns and go fast, your boot should have more forward flex. The backs should always have enough support so you can lever off of them if you need to. If you are more the slalom ace and just love to zeke turns on ice, you need a "muscle boot," with lots of stiffness with little fore-and-aft play. All forward motion of the shin into the boot is transmitted to the ski. I was amused to find the fit kit on my new five-buckle Koflach 612 SREs consisted solely of a rivet assembly to bolt the back of the cuff to the lower shell if I wanted a little more stiffness. Conan might like this boot. In general, a softer boot will handle more conditions than a stiffer one. If, after adjustment, the boot is still too stiff, shave the lower buckle on the cuff so it doesn't impinge on the lower shell.

FORWARD LEAN. Most boots have a forward flex adjustment. The torsionally stiff slalom skis get great edge bite with side-to-side edging movements and don't need a lot of weight up on the tips. A more upright angle in the boots works well. Starting with a more upright angle, you also have a greater range of motion in the ankle. Torsionally softer cruising skis often need more forward pressure on the tips, so a bit more forward lean is called for, though the quads need to be strong to accommodate permanent forward knee flexion. Tall skiers like a little more forward lean to lower their center of mass and increase their stability. The only way to know how much lean you need is by experimenting.

WOMEN'S BOOTS. Women have special boot needs. They have relatively larger calf muscles than men, so the leg flares abruptly. The average woman needs a boot cut down a little lower with a wide cuff at the top. She also tends to have a higher instep, narrower heel, and wider forefoot than a man.

Boot manufacturers have developed some very fine women's boots, though others have simply softened up some men's boots and colored them white. Some very good female skiers have spurned women's boots, however, because they felt they required the burlier men's models. Still, in many cases, the better fit from women's boots will increase performance. Whatever you select, there are a couple of other things for women to keep in mind. Because of the wider pelvis, a woman tends to ski in a knock-kneed position and pronate in the feet. She stands on her inside edge, and during turns tucks the knee of the downhill leg in behind the knee of the uphill leg, which inhibits freedom of movement. Additionally, a woman's center of mass is slightly rearward of a man's. The large calf muscles, along with the regular wearing of high heels, reduce ankle flexibility. When a woman's heel is down in the boot, she feels uncomfortably back on the skis, in a poor position to press forward. Since the ankle and the knee won't flex, she must bend at the waist to get forward.

To solve these problems, the shaft of the boot must be properly aligned, and if necessary, the boot must be canted; orthotics eliminate pronation, or inward rolling of the foot. Women particularly benefit from skiing with a wider foot position to avoid knee tuck. To get them comfortably forward on the ski and allow ankle flexion, there are heel lifts ranging from a half-inch to one inch. If this causes pressure on the foot because of a high instep, material can be ground out under the foot bed to drop the forefoot. Finally, consider mounting the binding slightly farther ahead than recommended, one to three centimeters.

LINERS. Any standard liner will pack down after a while, so get as snug a fit as possible without discomfort. As the liner flattens out, most performance skiers secure some pads to the shell or liner to retain the snugness. They're available with self-adhering backs. Felt pads are good because they don't compress. Foam rubber may flatten out faster than your liners did.

FOAMING. If you want to really lock your foot in, get your boots foamed. Most manufacturers offer an optional foam liner for their high-end boots. Foamed boots conform perfectly to *your* feet, are a little more rigid, do not compress over time, may outlast the shell, and provide better feel for the ski and snow. Foam liners also are more expensive, don't insulate as well, and are impossible to sell secondhand.

To foam a boot, the stockinged foot is placed in a plastic bag and put in the boot. The skier stands with his toes on a two-by-four to keep his heels well back in the heel pocket. A bottle of foaming agent is mixed with a catalyst, then affixed to injection tubes on top of the boot. The foam is forced into the liner and excess escapes through overflow tubes. To ensure proper distribution, the technician should open and close the buckles a few times as the foam flows through the liner before closing the buckles down. The foaming process can be fairly uncomfortable, since the chemical reaction produces heat, and the foam initially overexpands before contracting back just a bit on cooling.

The skier needs to remain in this position for at least fifteen minutes after injection. I've seen grown men cry; one actually passed out.

You can foam your own boots, but it's not recommended. If you get a pinched overflow tube and the foam bottle blows off, kiss your new $200 liners goodbye; you only get one chance to do it right. You can alleviate pressure points in a foam liner by carefully grinding it on a belt sander. Afterward, just slap some duct tape over the grind. You can also inject a drop of acetone with a hypodermic into the hot spot to dissolve the foam. Orthotics are a must for skiers who foam their boots.

ORTHOTICS. Your boot purchase is only the first step. You can tell immediately if your foot is slipping around in your boot; you will feel desperately out of control. Pads can solve the problem. The situation becomes a little more difficult when your boot fits snugly enough but you still lack control because of the biomechanics of the foot.

Walk across a hillside in your bare feet, and they will conform to the hill; no problem. When you traverse a hill on skis, what happens? If your edges are holding and you're not skidding, your feet are rigid levelers. You may be too accustomed to pronation when walking to notice it, but in your boot, it shows in that you can't get a direct response to the ski. Pronation has to take up the slack in the foot before the pressure is applied. The common quick fix is to crank the buckles down, but that cramps the foot or puts it to sleep.

Another common problem is pain in the ''sixth toe'' area on the outer ridge of the foot. In an attempt to relieve pressure, the skier gets the boot punched in that area, but the pain is unremitting. The unsupported foot rolls the outer edge up to hit the boot. If the boot is punched further, there is more space in which the painful point can rock around. Knee problems also can come from overpronation. The solution for all is to immobilize the foot with orthotics. They may be rigid for support or soft for comfort. Orthotics keep the foot from rolling, migrating, collapsing, and elongating, and allows solid energy transfer to the ski through the skeleton. Boot fitters say 80% of skiers would benefit from supportive orthotics and all would enjoy the added comfort.

There are two rigid orthotic systems: weight-bearing, produced by Superfeet; and non-weight-bearing, whose largest manufacturer is Peterson. There are other similar systems. In both cases, a rigid plastic blank is heated and an impression is made of the foot. In the weight-bearing system, the shape is formed while the foot is pressured. The blank is placed on a foam pillow, and the skier steps onto the pillow. This forces the blank around the foot while the skier's knees are held in cups on a metal stand and a plumb bob is used to align the legs. The orthotic is then posted (additional material is laminated under it and ground flat to seat into the bed of the boot) to create a stable base.

In the non-weight-bearing system, the skier sits while the foot hangs free. The rear foot is held by the technician in a neutral position, aligned with the shaft of the lower leg and knee. The impression is made by placing a cork blank in a plate that is shaped like the interior of a boot and secured to the foot. Then the foot is placed in a plastic bag. As the air is pumped out of the bag, the orthotic is vacuum-molded against the sole. Because it is unweighted, no flattening of the arch or inward rolling of the forefoot is allowed. As you

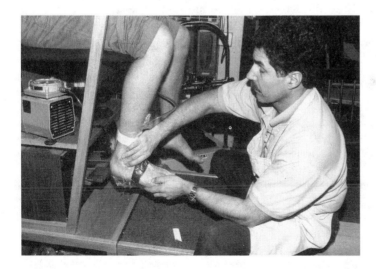

An orthotic stabilizes the skier's foot, preventing it from rolling, flattening, or elongating under pressure. Steve Forsythe, boot-fitting technician for Sturtevant's Sports in Seattle, aligns a customer's ankle in preparation for the molding process.

Boot shafts must precisely follow the natural orientation of the wearer's lower leg.

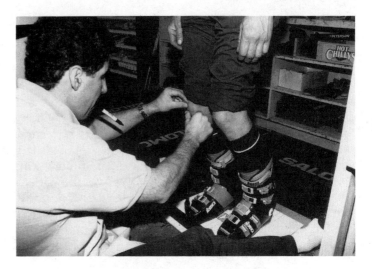

might imagine, there is a debate about the merits of each system, with fitters and marketers lined up on both sides. Ask questions at a specialty shop to determine which is best for you.

When the orthotic is finished, you should be able to stand on it and feel no high or low spots or wobble. It should not deform the liner in any way. In some cases, initial discomfort can be eliminated with some grinding or trimming by the technician. After having orthotics made to level your feet in your boots, you should have the boots balanced or set up so your lower leg does not push the boot in or out. This is done first with boot shaft alignment, then with canting if more adjustment is needed.

SHAFT ALIGNMENT. Almost all boots have some device, usually a screw or bolt at the ankle hinge, with which to adjust the shaft for bowlegged or knock-kneed skiers. If a skier is slightly bowlegged because the boot shaft is rigid, when he stands on a flat surface, the knees are forced together so he now appears knock-kneed. He must use more inward knee movement to get an edge, which stresses the knee. Conversely, knock-kneed skiers wearing boots on a flat surface appear bowlegged.

Women, in particular, ski in a knock-kneed position. Because of the wide hips, the femur angles outward and the tibia angles back inward to compensate. When standing with skis flat on the ground, the boots force the knees together, and again, solid edging is difficult. Women's boot shafts usually must be angled to the outside. Adjustment of the shaft is frequently called canting, but *canting* properly refers only to the addition of shims to tilt the foot inward or outward.

If your boots are unbalanced for your leg shape (even though your feet are level in the boots, in a normal skiing stance), you will ride on one of your edges. Many skiers can be seen with one ski flat on the snow and the other inverted or everted.

It does not take much angle either way to cause problems and there are some symptoms of unbalanced boots:

Inverted. If the boot shafts lean too much to the outside for the leg orientation, when the skier stands straight-legged in a normal skiing stance, the lower leg pushes the boot shaft to the inside, and the skier rides on his inside edges or has to ski bowlegged to compensate. This skier may make slight double turns before committing into the fall line. The arc at the top of the turn will wander. He finds that the ski may not finish through the turn because he has too high of an edge angle. The ski may rail out and head straight down the fall line.

In a turn, the skier has enough edge to pressure the ski and bend it, but he stands too straight, losing the advantage of lining the bones up to get the mechanical advantage of the skeletal structure. To compensate, he leans his body to the inside of the turn. At the end, he has to transfer his weight onto the uphill ski too early as the ski continues to arc around.

Everted. When the boot shaft leans too much to the inside for the orientation of the leg, the skier rides on his outside edges or must ski knock-kneed to compensate. The uphill ski rails out and continues to traverse the hill instead of entering into the new turn. To get adequate edge, the legs must be extended too far away from the upper body. Skis skid frequently in turns. Boots bruise the inside of the opposite knee because the boots have to be leaned too much to the inside to get sufficient edge.

There are several adjustment methods. A boot fitter should do this to ensure proper positioning. Most performance boots have an adjuster, usually only on the outboard side. Some, such as upper-end Raichle and Koflach boots, have adjustments on both sides to avoid pinching the shell on the inboard side.

There are several ways to check and change boot alignment. Remove the liner and place the orthotic in the bottom of the boot. Stand in the boot and place your feet comfortably apart and flex the knees in a normal skiing stance. Your feet should be no farther apart than hip width. In this way, your foot is aligned directly under your hip joint for maximum skeletal support. Because liners are symmetrical around the cuff, you should have equal distance from the cuff to the lower leg all the way around. You can reinsert the liners, loosen the adjustment, and walk around for a few minutes, going up and down some stairs. Then reassume your stance and tighten the adjustment. Remove the liners and recheck for equal leg cuff distance. A bob suspended from the center mass of the knee (not to be confused with the center of the kneecap) should fall to the center line of the boot.

According to preference, some slight adjustment inward or outward is acceptable. If you make short, quick turns all day, you might want to be slightly overcanted, so the bob falls slightly to the outside of the boot center line. With this adjustment, just a little inward knee movement puts you immediately on edge. For long turns, adjust for slight undercanting so the bob falls a bit to the inside. This way, you can get your legs farther away from you and drop your hips to the inside a little deeper.

CANTING. If alignment of the boot shaft is insufficient to get the skis flat on the snow, add cants. For a long time, they were plastic shims that were placed on the ski, then the binding would be mounted through them. Fortunately, this is fast disappearing. First, once you were used to this position, you could not easily try other skis, because they aren't similarly adjusted. Second, this system alters the left and right release function of the binding.

It is much better to add the cant inside the boot. Strips of plastic or tape can be positioned between the foot bed and the liner. Boot soles also can be ground, but this is not recommended. Few shops will do this for canting purposes because it changes the boot-binding release. Occasionally, a grinding may be warranted if you walk in the boots a lot and the sole is worn or warped, but it would be better to throw them away at that point. If you must walk in your boots, get some Cat Tracks for the soles.

Watch your knees and back after having boots leveled or balanced. Sometimes your body may resist realignment and give you some pain. In this case, reduce the amount of adjustment.

Mounting

Bindings need to be mounted by certified technicians. Over the years, the industry has worked hard to ensure that the boot-binding system is as safe as can be. After bindings, whether new or used, are mounted, the system is tested for function, and release values must fall within specified norms. Today, home binding mounts are as smart as home dentistry. Shops won't mount pre-Deutsche Industrial Norm (DIN) standard bindings.

Boots are marked at a point usually half the distance of the foot, though in some cases, it's the halfway position of the sole. The mark is the point on the ski where the center boot mark should match.

Some skiers ignore the mark and determine the mounting point by measuring the chord length of the ski—the straight-line length from tip to tail—and using the halfway point, or one centimeter ahead, as the toe position. This may have been okay a few years ago, but not now. Manufacturers mark the ski according to several factors, including the position of the center of the side cut. Some skis have modified tips, such as the Rossignol Quantum, which changes the swing-weight center, affecting positioning. This is only in the case of boots larger than size eleven or smaller than size six. Ask a technician or manufacturer's representative for a recommendation. Racers may want to mount their slalom skis ahead by a centimeter or so, and downhillers, slightly back.

Poles

Poles announce the beginning of most turns. They are pretty simple. Other than some with a corrective angle near the grip, the only variable to consider is the grade. Most poles are of aluminum alloy. The strongest are made of 7000 series aluminum, and are more expensive than 6000 or 5000 series. The 7001 series is the lightest and strongest, though 7075 aluminum may not be as brittle. On the upper-end poles, the grade is usually marked on the shaft.

Swing weight is important. If you are deciding between two poles, swing them both at the same time. The lighter pole will oscillate more than the heavier one.

Racers prefer the pistol grip for more range of motion. The grips with large tops are designed to prevent punching yourself in the eye with a small surface area. If venturing out to a ridge for some backcountry skiing, you will want pole straps to help you get a good push.

A good pole may cost $65. If price is no object, ones made of graphite can run more than $150. Graphite poles can stand much greater stress than aluminum ones, though they can be more susceptible to edge nicks and cuts.

Bibliography

ONE   The Challenge of Skiing Today

Editorial Staff. "Ski Technique in the 1990s." *Snow Country.* March 1990. p. 18.

The Editors. "Interview with Leo Lacroix." *Ski Tech.* September/October 1988. p. 60.

TWO   Physical Fitness for Skiers

Astrand, Per-Olof, and Rodahl, Kaare. *Textbook of Work Physiology: Physiological Bases of Exercise.* McGraw-Hill Book Co., New York, N.Y. 1986.

Bonnevie, Ron. "Energy Sources in Alpine Skiing, and Energy Cost of and Energy Sources for Alpine Skiing in Top Athletes." *American Ski Coach.* Volume 10, Number 5, May 1987. pp. 20–21.

Dudley, Gary A., and Fleck, Steven J. "Strength and Endurance Training: Are They Mutually Exclusive?" *American Ski Coach.* Volume 11, Number 2, November 1987. p. 23.

Duvillard, Serge, Ph.D. "Lactate Threshold: An Important Concept in Competitive Alpine Skiing." *American Ski Coach.* Volume 11, Number 3. January 1988. p. 33.

Eriksson, Forsberg, Nilsson, and Karlsson. *Muscle

Strength, EMG Activity and Oxygen Uptake During Downhill Skiing. National Defence Research Institute, Stockholm, Sweden.

Fixx, James F. *Maximum Sports Performance.* Random House, New York, N.Y. 1985.

Fox, Edward L.; Kirby, Timothy E.; Fox, Ann Roberts. *Bases of Fitness.* Macmillan Publishing Co., New York, N.Y. 1987.

Gilmore, C. P. *Exercising for Fitness.* Time-Life Books, Alexandria, Virginia. 1981.

Graetzer, Dan. "The Symptoms of Overtraining." *Sports Guide.* December 1989. p. 38.

Howley, Edward T., and Franks, B. Don. *Health/ Fitness Instructor's Handbook.* Human Kinetics Publishers, Inc., Champaign, Illinois. 1986.

Koerber, William. "Motor Skills Learning and the Teaching of Skiing." *Journal of Professional Ski Instruction.* March 1983. p. 28.

LaVallee, Tim. "Strength Training and Ski Performance." *American Ski Coach.* Volume 10, Number 5. May 1987. p. 24.

Margreiter, Werner. "The Complexity of Motor Skills." *American Ski Coach.* Volume 12, Number 4. Summer 1988. p. 10.

Marshall, Bruce (publisher). *Muscles: The Magic of Motion.* Torstar Books Inc., New York, N.Y. 1985.

Perrine, Jim, and Copeland, Jack. "More Specific Muscle Preparation for Alpine Skiing." *Professional Skier.* Winter II, p. 44; and III, p. 37. 1986.

Smith, Doug. "Power Skiers." *The Professional Skier.* Winter III, 1989. p. 24.

Smith, Doug; Rauch, Andreas; Mayr, Klaus. "Error Diagnosis." *The Professional Skier.* Winter I, 1989. pp. 34–41.

Stray-Gunderson, Jim. "Anaerobic Threshold: An Attractive Myth." *Journal of Professional Ski Instruction.* December 1984. p. 31.

Twardokens, George. "The Skier's Structure, Function and Performance at a Glance." *American Ski Coach.* Volume 12, Number 1. Autumn 1988.

Wessel, Janet A. *Movement Fundamentals: Figure, Form, Fun.* Prentice Hall, Englewood Cliffs, New Jersey. 1970.

THREE   Fitness Testing

American College of Sports Medicine. *Guidelines for Exercise Testing and Prescription.* Lea and Febiger, Philadelphia, Pennsylvania. 1986.

Mathews, Donald K., and Fix, Edward L. *The Physiological Basis of Physical Education and Athletics.* W. B. Saunders Co., Philadelphia, Pennsylvania. 1976.

National Alpine Staff. *U.S. Ski Team Alpine Training Manual.* U.S. Ski Team, Box 100, Park City, Utah. 1985.

Sleamaker, Rob. *Serious Training for Serious Athletes.* Leisure Press, Champaign, Illinois. 1989.

FOUR   Flexibility

Anderson, Bob. *Stretching.* Shelter Publications, Inc., Bolinas, California. 1980.

Gallwey, Timothy, and Kriegel, Bob. *Inner Skiing.* Bantam Books, New York, N.Y. 1985.

FIVE   Boot Camp for Snow Warriors

Costill, David L., Ph.D. "A Scientific Approach to Distance Running." *Track and Field News.* 1981.

Graetzer, Dan. "Plyometrics for Explosive Speed." *Sports Guide.* Volume 8, Number 2. February 1990. p. 36.

Liquori, Marty. *Real Running.* Playboy Paperbacks, Chicago, Illinois. 1980.

SIX   Skiing Strength

James, Don, and Huegli, Rick. *Conditioning for Football the University of Washington Way.* Leisure Press, West Point, N.Y. 1982.

LaVallee, Tim. "Building a Good Set of Wheels." *American Ski Coach.* Volume 10, Number 5. May 1987. p. 27.

LaVallee, Tim. "Strength Training and Ski Performance." *American Ski Coach.* Volume 10, Number 5. May 1987. p. 24.

Malyszko, Michael. "Pumping Iron With Archimedes." *Technology Illustrated.* April 1983. p. 39.

Mathews, Donald K., and Fix, Edward L. *The Physiological Basis of Physical Education and Athletics.*

W. B. Saunders Co., Philadelphia, Pennsylvania. 1976.

Nelson, Janet. "Muscle Building the Girardelli Way." *Ski.* January 1989. p. 28.

Thompson, Clem W. *Manual of Structural Kinesiology.* Times Mirror/Mosby College Publishing. 1985.

Wayne, Rick. "To Squat or Not to Squat." *Flex.* July 1987. p. 22.

SEVEN   When the Snow's Gone

Hughes, Charles. *Soccer Tactics and Teamwork.* EP Publishing Ltd., West Yorkshire, England. 1981.

Tohei, Koichi. *Ki in Daily Life.* Ki No Kenkyukai, Tokyo, Japan. 1980.

U'Ren, Steve. *Performance Kayaking.* Stackpole Books, Harrisburg, Pennsylvania. 1989.

Westbrook, A., and Ratti, O. *Aikido and the Dynamic Sphere.* Charles Tuttle and Co., Rutland, Vermont. 1980.

EIGHT   Training Plans

Bompa, Tudor. *Theory and Methodology of Training.* Kendall/Hunt, Dubuque, Iowa. 1985.

Duvillard, Serge. "Training Periods, Training Cycles and Intensity in Competitive Alpine Skiing." *Journal of Professional Ski Coaching and Instruction.* September 1984. p. 57.

Hagerman, Gene, and McMurtry, John. "An Alpine Training Program." *American Ski Coach.* Volume 11, Number 1. September 1987. p. 27.

LaVallee, Tim. "Theory of Training: A Key to Athletic Performance." *American Ski Coach.* Volume 11, Number 1. September 1987. p. 21.

NINE   The Basic Turn

Armstrong, John. "Why Do We Stress Weighting the Outside Ski in a Turn?" *American Ski Coach.* Volume 10, Number 5. May 1987. p. 14.

Campbell, Stu. "Breakthrough." *Ski.* January 1988. p. 57.

Howe, John. *Skiing Mechanics.* Poudre Press, La Porte, Colorado. 1982.

Jenson, Sidney L., Ph.D. "Perpendicularity: Skiing's two right-angled movements." *Journal of Profes-*

sional Ski Coaching and Instruction. September 1985. p. 71.

LaVallee, Tim. "Technique. Bamboo vs. Flex Poles." *American Ski Coach.* Volume 10, Number 13. p. 12.

Larsson, Olle, "Learn From the Best." *Skiing.* February 1990. p. 88.

Smith, Doug. "Turn Initiation Technique." *The Professional Skier.* Winter III, 1987. p. 16.

TEN   Skiing Drills on Your Own

National Alpine Staff. *U.S. Ski Team Alpine Training Manual.* U.S. Ski Team, Box 100, Park City, Utah. 1985.

PSIA Steering Committee. *The American Teaching System: Strategies for Teaching.* Publisher's Press, Salt Lake City, Utah. 1987.

ELEVEN   Racing Basics

Capaul, George. Lecture on slalom technique. National Coaches Camp, Mount Bachelor, Oregon. Spring 1988.

Capaul, George. "Modern Slalom Technique and Edging Drills." *American Ski Coach.* Volume 12, Number 4. p. 2.

Karlsson, Torbjorn. Lecture on slalom and GS technique. National Coaches Conditioning Symposium, Park City, Utah. 1990.

Lange, Serge. *21 Years of World Cup Racing.* Johnson Books, Boulder, Colorado. 1986.

Mahre, Phil and Steve. *No Hill Too Fast.* Simon and Schuster, New York, New York. 1985.

Major, Paul. "A Study of Giant Slalom Skiing." *American Ski Coach.* Volume 13, Number 1. Winter 1990. p. 26.

Major, James, and Larson, Olle. *World Cup Ski Technique.* Poudre Press, La Porte, Colorado. 1979.

TWELVE   Tech Talk: Your Gear

Davignon, Al. "Designing a World Cup Ski." *The Journal of Professional Ski Coaching and Instruction.* March 1983. p. 18.

Davignon, Al. "Ski Vibrations." *The Journal of Professional Ski Coaching and Instruction.* December 1984. p. 16.

Davignon, Al. "Design for Damping." *The Professional Skier.* Winter 1986. p. 27.

Gleason. Bob. "Boot Basics." *Ski Tech.* November/December 1988. p. 16.

Howden, Michael. *World Class Ski Tuning.* WCST Publishing, Portland, Oregon. 1985.

Kiesel, Rob. "Heat, Pressure, Time." *Ski Tech.* November/December 1986. p. 20.

Mossman, Linda. "The Elements of Canting." *American Ski Coach.* Volume 13, Number 3. Summer 1990. p. 7.

Nelson, Janet. "Is Your Ski Equipment Sexist?" *Ski.* October 1983. p. 90.

Pfeifer, Luanne. "The Basic Pole Plays a Role." *Ski Tech.* November/December 1986. p. 44.

Schultes, Hermann. *The Alpine Ski.* Olin Ski Company, Middleton, Connecticut. 1980.

Timmons, Kelly. *Advanced Bootfitting.* Ski Retailers Workshops Training Manual. Ski Business, Alaco Productions, Ltd., Chicago, Illinois. 1990.

Whiting, Russ. "Suppliers Target Tuning." *Ski Tech.* October 1990. p. 16.

Index